SCHIRMER PERFORMANCE EDITIONS

HAL LEONARD PIANO LIBRARY

CLEMENTI

SONATINAS

Opus 36

Edited by Jennifer Linn

Also available:
00296466 Clementi: Sonatinas, Opus 36,
with companion recordings by Jennifer Linn

On the cover:
The New Spinet
by George Goodwin Kilburne
(1839-1924)

ISBN 978-1-4950-0727-9

G. SCHIRMER, *Inc.*

DISTRIBUTED BY

7777 W. BLUEMOUND RD. P.O. BOX 13819 MILWAUKEE, WI 53213

www.musicsalesclassical.com
www.halleonard.com

LABORUM
DULCE
LENIMEN
G. SCHIRMER

CONTENTS

HISTORICAL NOTES

Muzio Clementi (1752-1832)

In Muzio Clementi's hands, the pianoforte eclipsed the harpsichord in popularity and a new school of piano playing was born. Clementi was among the world's first piano virtuosos, one of several Classical-era composers who helped create the piano sonata, and the first composer to write expressly for the properties of the new pianoforte. A highly regarded teacher and conductor, he was also an astute businessman who manufactured pianos and ran an international music publishing business.

Clementi was born in Rome, began his musical studies at a young age, and became organist at his own church at age 13. When he was 14, a wealthy British man named Peter Beckford "bought" him for a term of seven years. This indentured servitude provided the young musician with a musical and academic education. In 1774, no longer obligated to Beckford, Clementi moved to London, where he began performing as a harpsichordist. However, the advancements made to the pianos of his time soon led him away from the older instrument.

In 1780 Clementi began a concert tour of Europe. On Christmas Eve 1781, Emperor Josef II of Austria staged a musical contest for the entertainment of his guests, pitting Clementi against another famous pianist of the era. The two players were required to improvise and to play some of their own compositions as well as those of other composers. The other competitor was none other than Mozart. The two were quite evenly matched as performers. Mozart was not at all happy about finding a pianistic equal. He made harsh, petty comments about Clementi in letters to his sister Nannerl, calling his colleague a "charlatan" and a "mere mechanicus" (machine). Clementi, however, had nothing but praise for Mozart, saying he had "never heard anyone play with such spirit and grace."

It was Clementi's work that helped define the sonata-allegro form, a single movement within a sonata (as well as within a symphony, string quartet, etc.) consisting of three sections: the exposition, or statement of the movement's principal themes; the development, in which the composer expands upon, alters, and combines the themes laid out in the exposition; and the recapitulation, in which the exposition is repeated with some changes. The recapitulation is often followed by a coda, which brings the piece to a tidy, decisive conclusion. Clementi's sonatas had an enormous impact on composers who would follow, including his younger contemporary Beethoven. Clementi's music foreshadows that of Beethoven, providing a bridge between the Classical and Romantic eras. Beethoven, for his part, had tremendous admiration for Clementi and borrowed the theme from the "Presto" movement of Clementi's Op. 13, No. 6 sonata for the final movement of his *Symphony No. 3, ("Eroica")*. Clementi's educational works, the *Six Progressive Sonatinas, Op. 36; Introduction to the Art of Playing on the Piano Forte*; and *Gradus ad Parnassum*, remain valued teaching tools today. He published the *Op. 36 Sonatinas* himself in 1797, revising them some 20 years later.

Clementi traveled throughout Europe during his career, but England remained his home. Although some of his travels were built around concert tours, others were intended to promote his business interests. He was away from England from 1802 to 1810, creating a market for his pianos and securing the publishing rights to music by various composers. After 1810, Clementi remained in England writing music and building pianos. He remained vigorous and remarkably healthy until the very last weeks of his life. He died on 10 March 1832, at age 80, and was buried in the cloisters of Westminster Abbey.

—Elaine Schmidt

PERFORMANCE NOTES

Sonatina No. 1: first movement, mm.1-18 (original edition)

(+ indicates the thumb; 1, 2, 3, 4 indicate the four fingers)

Muzio Clementi composed the *Six Progressive Sonatinas, Op. 36* in 1797 and recommended them for use as supplementary material in his landmark publication *Introduction to the Art of Playing on the Piano Forte* (1801). Because no autograph has ever been found, this first edition serves as the most original source for authentic score study. It is not without obvious notational errors and omissions, however, and calls upon the performer to understand detailed performance practices and nuances, especially concerning articulation and ornamentation. My goal has been to provide an edition for students and teachers that is accurate and faithful to the original intent of the composer, but which provides the necessary stylistic editorial additions to help them achieve the most authentic and musical performance possible.

Even now, virtually no pianist's training would be complete without studying these first steps of the classical repertoire, more than 200 years after their debut. Without doubt, their lasting popularity is due to a proven success in developing the pianist's technique and stylistic understanding. True to his title, "Father of the Pianoforte," Clementi understood the young students who would be learning his pieces. In the first few sonatinas of Op. 36, he wrote them with a simpler coordination between the hands, but then proceeded skillfully to include more complicated accompaniment patterns and ornamentation in the later ones. He kept musical reaches all within the span of an octave as well as fingering them for a child's hand rather than his own. These gems of the sonatina genre are beautifully accessible music that sound authentic and real. Amazingly and without oversimplification, Clementi was able to create these miniatures of Classical style for the pianistic delight of generations to come.

Articulation

The various touches and articulations described in quotations below are taken from Clementi's *Introduction to the Art of Playing on the Piano Forte.*

SLUR

"called LEGATO in Italian, must be played in a SMOOTH and CLOSE manner"

It is interesting to note that, in the first published edition, the first movement of Op. 36, No. 1 contained no slurs. However, this did not mean that the passages were to be played without *legato* and *staccato* articulation. We can look again to Clementi's instruction: "When the composer leaves the LEGATO, and STACCATO to the performer's taste; the best rule is, to adhere chiefly to the LEGATO; reserving the STACCATO to give SPIRIT occasionally to certain passages, and to set off the HIGHER BEAUTIES of the LEGATO."

The first slur in Op. 36 appears in the second movement of Sonatina No. 1 (original edition).

***Sonatina No. 1:* second movement, mm. 7-8**

Should the *legato* touch be broken each time a slur ends? In her landmark book *Performance Practices in Classic Piano Music*, Sandra Rosenblum states, "The answer is yes much of the time, because of the finesse imparted to the line by appropriate accentuation and articulation." She describes a similar slurring situation: "... the end of the slur must be all but imperceptible, sometimes heard more as a lightness than as a separation..." This does not mean however, that all slur endings always indicate a definite release. In certain circumstances, the *legato* touch may extend over the barline even though the slur itself does not.

> This idiosyncratic Classic slurring occurs most commonly in four categories: a short motive slurred as one unit within a measure, but not when it crosses a bar line; a trill with written-out termination whose slur ends before the note that follows; successive measure-length slurs; and successive slurs that stop and start over a *cantabile* melody in unexpected places.[1]

***Sonatina No. 5:* second movement, mm. 3-5**

Original edition

New Schirmer edition

Slurs were also used to create rhythmic emphasis on a normally weak beat; they were especially expressive when used over repeating patterns. In the Rondo movement of *Sonatina No. 5*, many editors have chosen either to omit the slur indications which begin on the second beat in mm. 34-35, or to add the original slur indications of mm. 34-35 to mm. 6-7 and all similar situations. The fact that slurs are added very sparingly in the original edition and that this expressive slurring does not occur in the original edition until m. 34 is significant. It suggests to me an interesting variation on a repeating pattern rather than a forgotten slur.

***Sonatina No. 5:* third movement, mm. 6-7**

***Sonatina No. 5:* third movement, mm. 34-35**

STACCATO

Wedge:

"called in ITALIAN, STACCATO; denoting DISTINCTNESS, and SHORTNESS of sound; which is produced by lifting the finger up, as soon as it has struck the key"

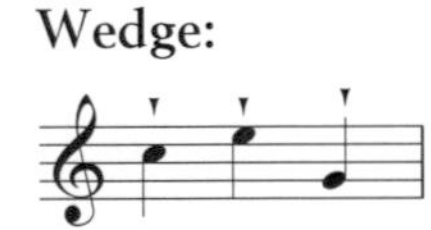

Dot: "or they are marked thus

which, when composers are EXACT in their writing, means LESS staccato than the preceding mark (wedge); the finger, therefore, is kept down somewhat longer"

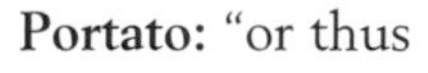

Portato: "or thus

which means STILL LESS staccato: the nice degrees of MORE and LESS, however, depend on the CHARACTER, and PASSION of the piece; the STYLE of which must be WELL OBSERVED by the performer"

Dynamics

The dynamic range of Clementi's pianoforte was limited in comparison to the powerful dynamic depth of the modern grand piano. The dynamic levels on the period instruments were approximately one level below our modern instruments. A genuine *forte* would register only as *mezzo forte*. With this knowledge, the performer must decide whether to play the modern instrument with its own true *forte* volume, or to hold back the tone slightly to achieve a more historical sound perspective. While it lies partly in the taste of the performer, it is desirable to take into consideration this historical approach when playing *forte*, always keeping the refined nature of the classical style in mind.

Pedaling

At the time these sonatinas were written, the damper pedal was an innovation to the pianoforte. Experimentation with the new sounds created by the "open dampers" was not usually indicated in the score, and the difference in the actual mechanisms (knee levers or foot pedals) left the performer with a choice as to how they would be used. Though sporadic, Clementi notated pedal indications in some of his keyboard works. He added pedal markings to the Op. 36 sonatinas in their fifth edition, published by his company ca. 1820. (See, for example, *Sonatina No. 3*: third movement, mm. 42-45; *Sonatina No. 5*: first movement, mm. 42-44.)[2]

Regarding the use of the damper pedal in the sonatinas, we should remember their educational nature and the ability of the performer or student to achieve the necessary nuances. Because of the quick natural decay of the tone on Clementi's instrument, the damper pedal would most likely be used in slow movements and on occasional cadence points or broken-chord passages. (See suggested pedal use in the following examples.)

***Sonatina No. 1:* second movement, mm. 1-3**

***Sonatina No. 3:* first movement, mm. 11-12**

Its use must be carefully placed; depending on the particulars of the modern instrument, one should consider depressing the pedal only one-half or one-quarter of its full depth. This will diminish the reverberation, keeping the sound more in line with the period instrument and the composer's intentions.

English Square Piano built by Clementi's firm, ca. 1796. Note the single (damper) pedal.

Ornamentation

The Appoggiatura

"The APPOGGIATURA is a GRACE prefixed to a note, which is always played LEGATO, and with more or less EMPHASIS; being derived from the ITALIAN verb APPOGGIARE, to LEAN UPON; and is written in a SMALL NOTE. Its LENGTH is borrowed from the following LARGE note and in GENERAL, it is half of its duration; MORE or LESS, however according to the EXPRESSION of the passage."

The *appoggiatura* first occurs in the Op. 36 set in the first and second movements of *Sonatina No. 3.*

Sonatina No. 3: first movement, m. 14

Sonatina No. 3: second movement, mm. 15-16

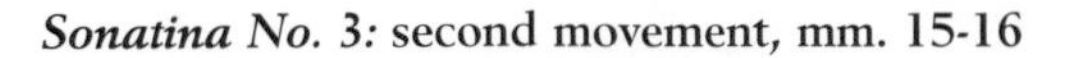

Although I prefer that the small note at the opening of *Sonatina No. 5* be played on the beat, this particular *appoggiatura*, because of its quick tempo, can be performed as an anticipatory grace note or as an *acciaccatura* in which the small note and main note sound virtually together. All of these realizations are in keeping with the performance practices of Clementi's day. The key words of the composer, "according to the EXPRESSION of the passage," certainly allow the pianist this kind of discretion.

Sonatina No. 5: first movement, mm. 1-2

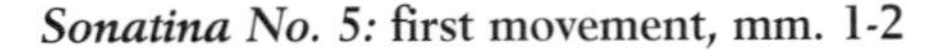

It is interesting to compare the two *appoggiaturas* below with regard to Clementi's instruction "to LEAN upon." In general, it is expected that the small note is emphasized (as in *Sonatina No. 5:* second movement, m.10), but in the case of the *Sonatina No. 6*, Clementi puts ***fz***, making it clear that the main note receives the emphasis. "Clementi placed the emphasis on the main note after 'little notes' that leap or that precede main notes approached by leap."[3]

Sonatina No. 5: second movement, mm. 10-11

Sonatina No. 6: first movement, mm. 1-2

The Slide

Op. 36 contains two movements with slides:

Sonatina No. 5: second movement, mm. 1-2

Sonatina No. 6: second movement, mm. 16-17

Given the somewhat moderate tempo (*Allegretto moderato*), it is appropriate to play the slide in *Sonatina No. 5* on the beat. The second movement of *Sonatina No. 6* is open to debate, however; because of the quick tempo of this movement (*Allegro spiritoso*), it is acceptable to play this slide before the beat, thereby emphasizing the principal note and natural pulse.

The Turn

In keeping with the progressive nature of the set, Clementi rightfully postponed the use of the turn until *Sonatina No. 4*. These ornaments should be played on the beat and generally within the harmonic context. Clementi states in his *Introduction to the Art of Playing on the Piano Forte*: "THE TURN The lowest note of *every* sort of turn is *mostly* a semi-tone."

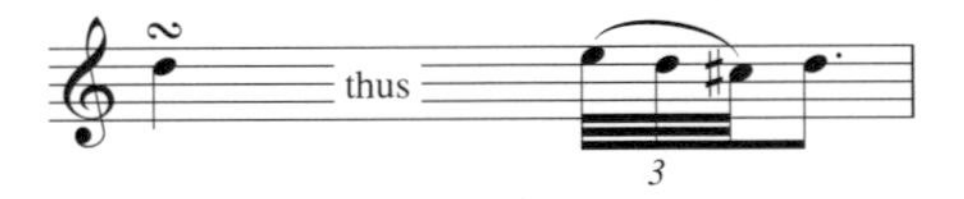

Rosenblum states, however, "The interval between the outer notes of a turn was almost always meant to be a minor third."[4] Therefore, the ornament in *Sonatina No. 4* (second movement, m. 31) could be realized with either G or G#. Neither the semitone nor the minor third suggestion seems to fit the turn in the second movement of *Sonatina No. 5;* given this particular context, fitting the notes of the turn within the C major framework is the most appropriate choice and can be supported in a similar ornamental situation in m. 10.

Sonatina No. 4: second movement, mm. 31-33

Sonatina No. 5: second movement, mm. 1-2

Sonatina No. 5: second movement, mm. 10-11

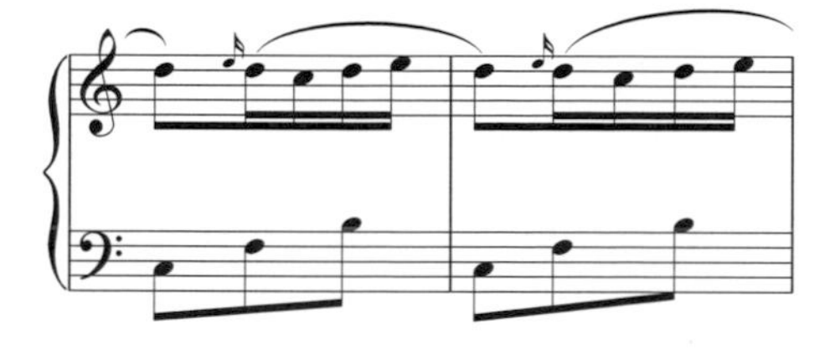

The Trill

Clementi states: "The GENERAL mark for the shake is this ***tr*** and composers trust CHIEFLY to the taste and judgment of the performer, whether it shall be long, short, transient, or turned." Rosenblum states, "Clementi also remained rather conservative, endorsing only the upper-note start except in a stepwise *legato* approach..."

Below are two examples in the Op. 36 sonatinas where the trill can begin on the principal note.

Sonatina No. 3: first movement, m. 56

Sonatina No. 5: first movement, mm. 22-23

Tempo

Choosing the appropriate tempo depends on the interpretation of the composer's tempo markings as well as the taste and ability of the performer. Rosenblum states, "for at least in 1801 Clementi considered *adagio* the slowest tempo. His order of terms, becoming faster, is *adagio, grave, largo, lento, larghetto, andantino,* and *andante*."[5]

In a letter from 1783, Mozart wrote "Clementi is a *ciarlatano*, like all Italians. He writes *Presto* over a sonata or even *Prestissimo* and *Alla breve*, and plays it himself *Allegro* in 4/4 time." Tempo preferences differed from region to region, and although Clementi certainly had the technical virtuosity to play at whatever speed possible, he perhaps preferred a more moderate *Presto*.

In the present edition, I have included metronome markings for each movement which represent a suggested range within the tempo, allowing for the ability and preference of the performer.

Fingering

Malcolm Bilson's measurements of Mozart's Viennese piano indicate a key dip of "about 3 millimeters and it takes roughly 10-15 grams to get it down." Our modern piano has a key depth of "about 9 millimeters and it takes roughly 55 grams to push it down."[6] With this comparison, it is understandable that some of Clementi's original fingerings are not practical on our modern instruments; it is therefore reasonable to adjust fingerings to the modern performer's instrument and current pedagogical practices.

References

1. Sandra Rosenblum, *Performance Practices in Classic Piano Music* (Bloomington: Indiana University Press, 1991), 175.
2. *Ibid.*, 130.
3. *Ibid.*, 222.
4. *Ibid.*, 261.
5. *Ibid.*, 352.
6. Malcolm Bilson, "Pianos in Mozart's Time" in *Piano Quarterly 86* (Summer 1974), 30.

Suggested Reading

Clementi, Muzio. *Introduction to the Art of Playing on the Piano Forte* (1801), ed. Sandra P. Rosenblum with New Introduction (1973). New York: Da Capo Press, 1974.

Plantinga, Leon. *Clementi: His Life and Music.* London: Oxford University Press, 1977.

Rosen, Charles. *The Classical Style: Haydn, Mozart, Beethoven.* New York: Viking Press, 1972.

Rosenblum, Sandra. *Performance Practices in Classic Piano Music.* Bloomington and Indianapolis: Indiana University Press, 1991.

Temperley, Nicholas (ed.). *The London Pianoforte School, 1766-1860.* New York: Garland, 1984-87.

—Jennifer Linn

Sonatina in C Major

I

Muzio Clementi
Op. 36, No. 1

Allegro [𝅗𝅥 = 80-100]

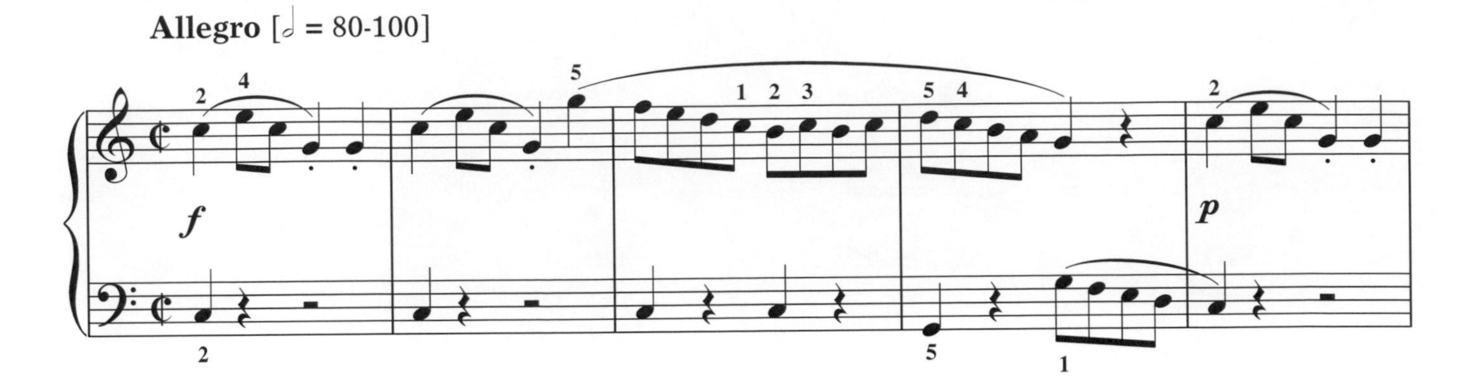

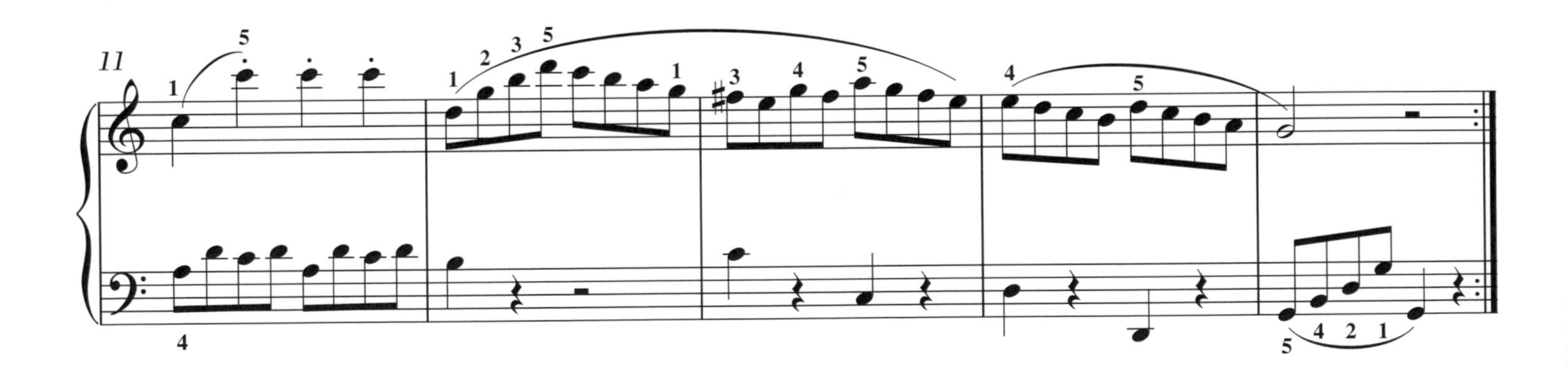

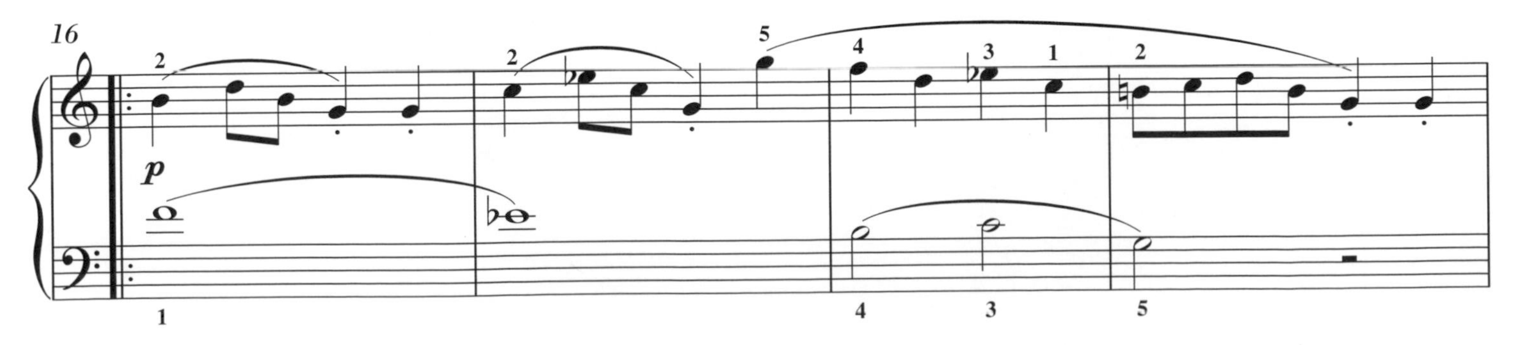

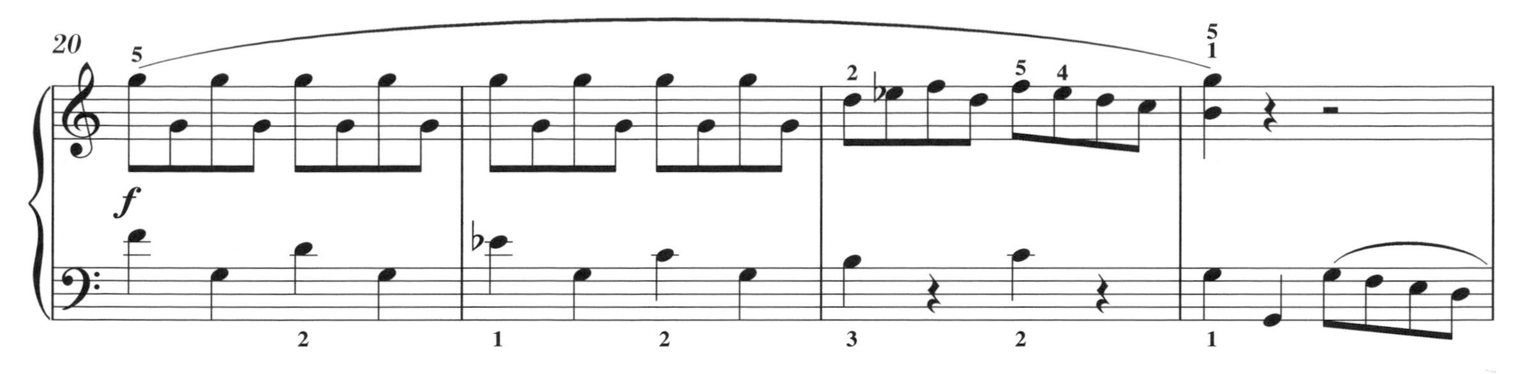
20
f

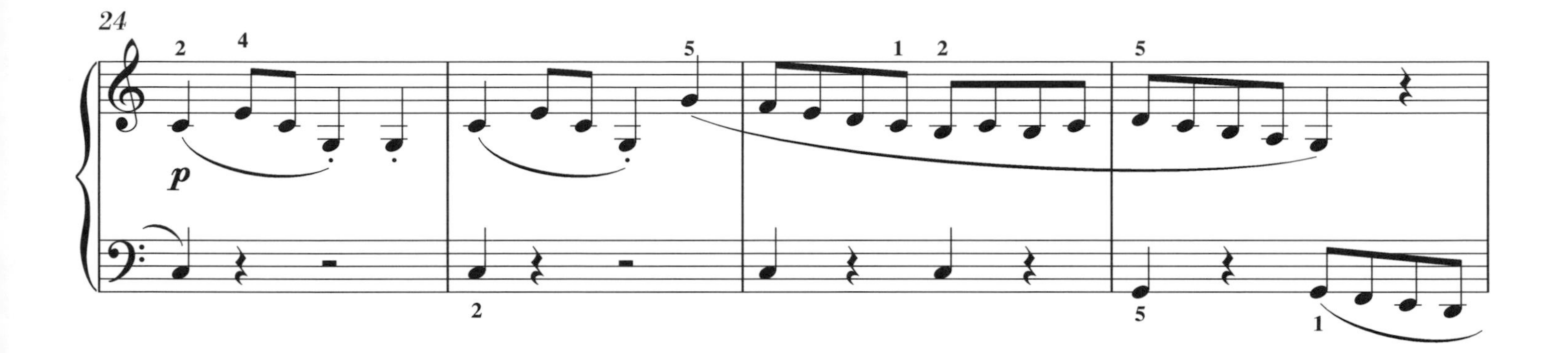
24
p

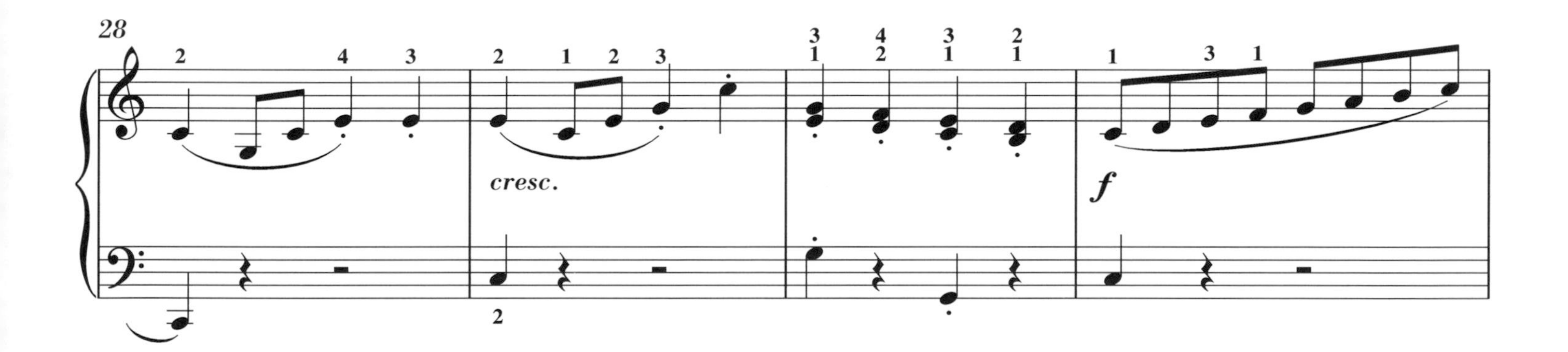
28
cresc.
f

32

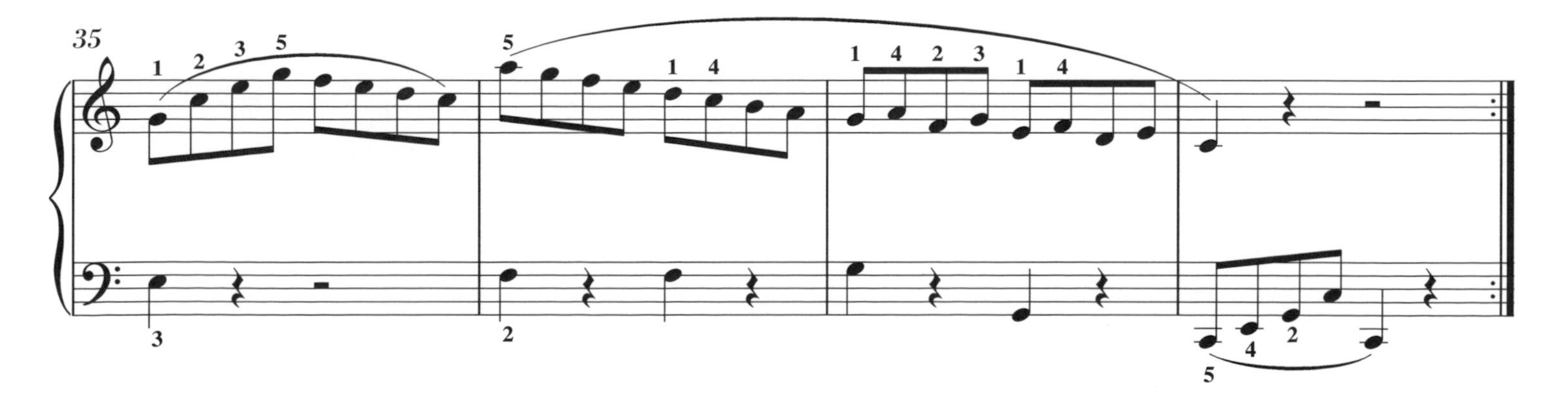
35

II

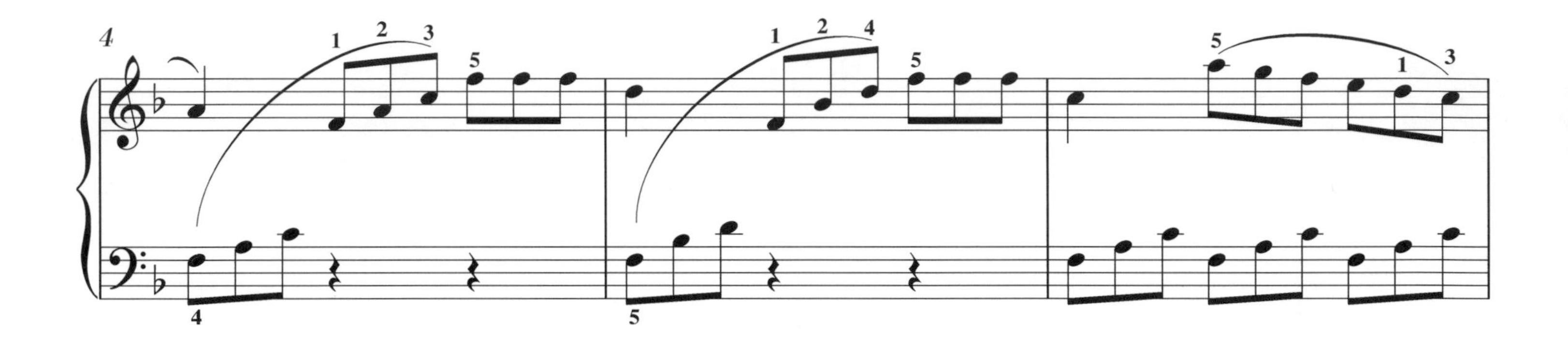

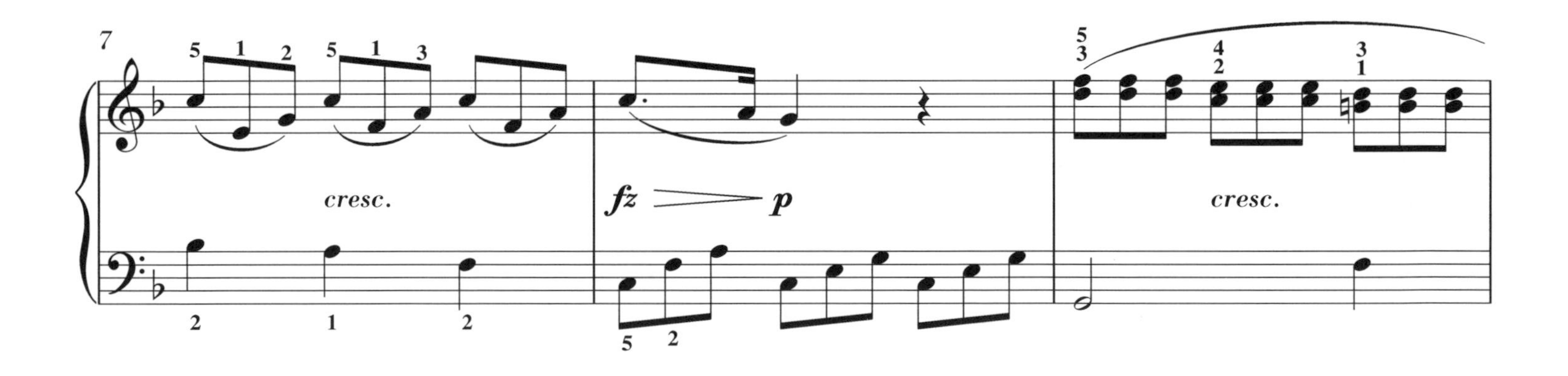

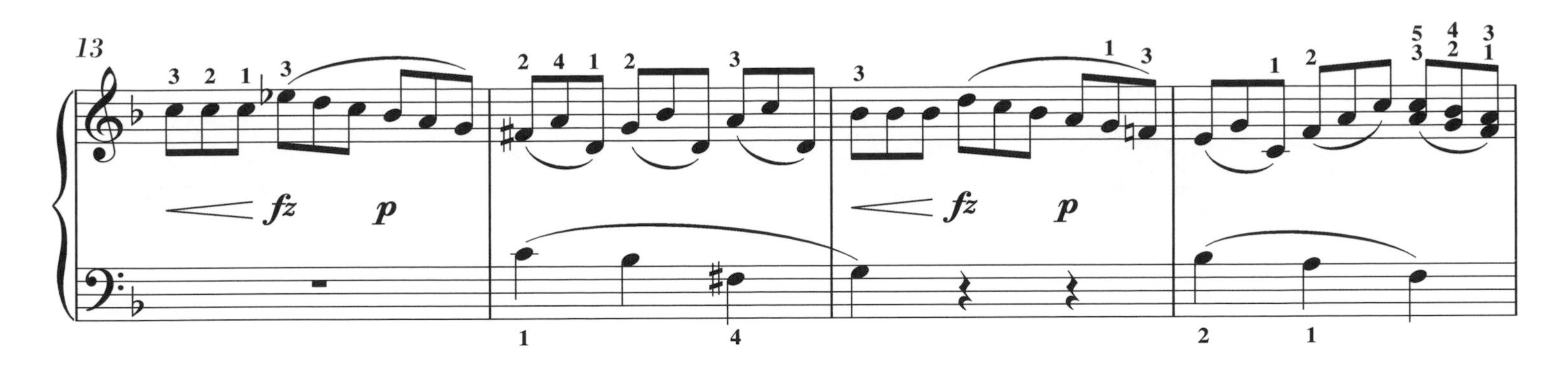
13
fz
p
fz
p

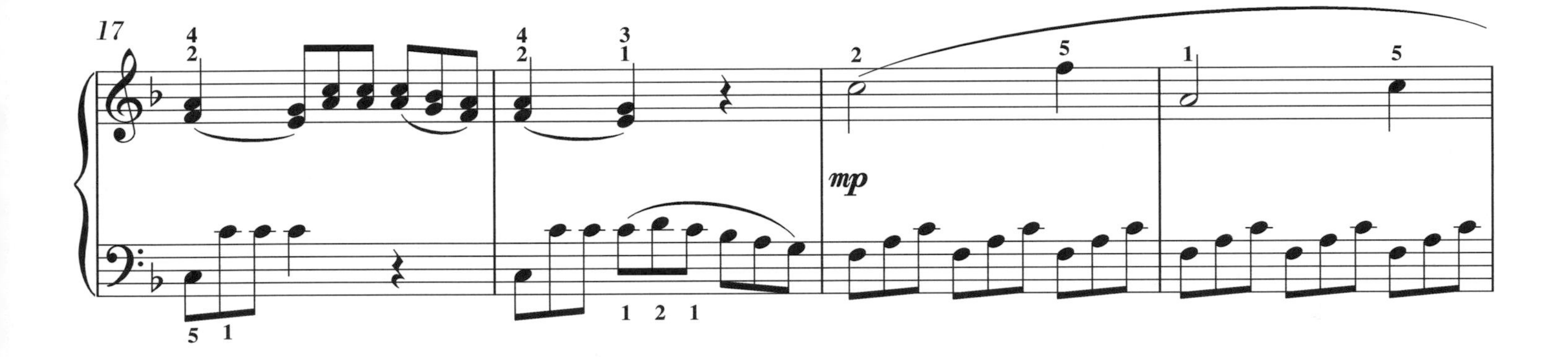
17
mp

21
tr
dim.
p
cresc.

24
f
tr

III

Vivace [♩. = 69-80]

p

legato

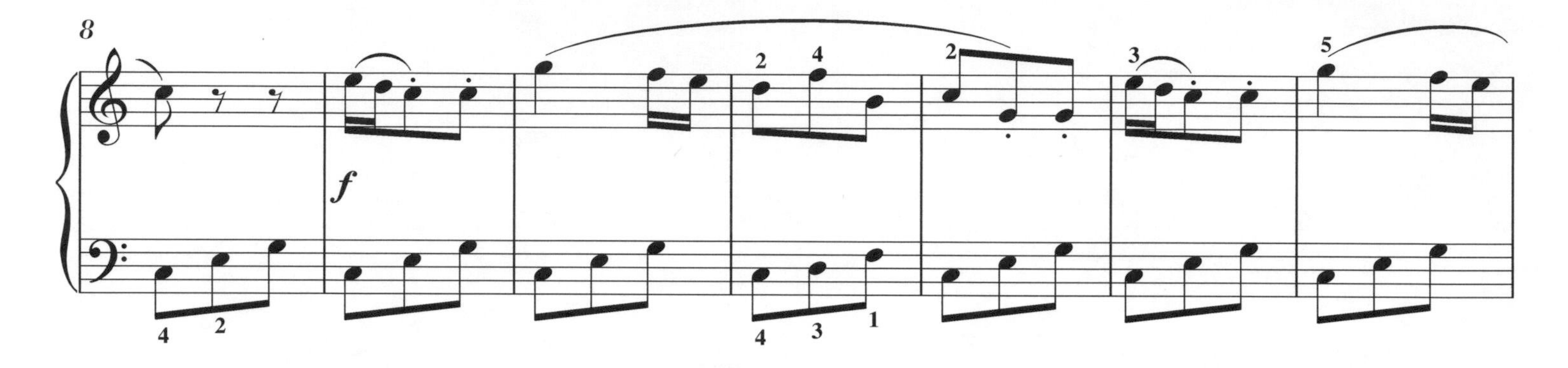

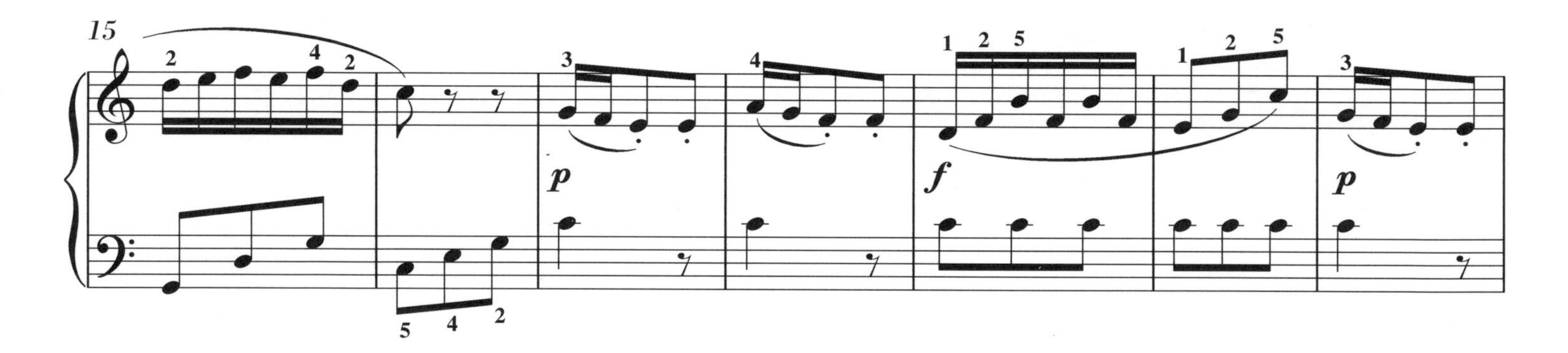

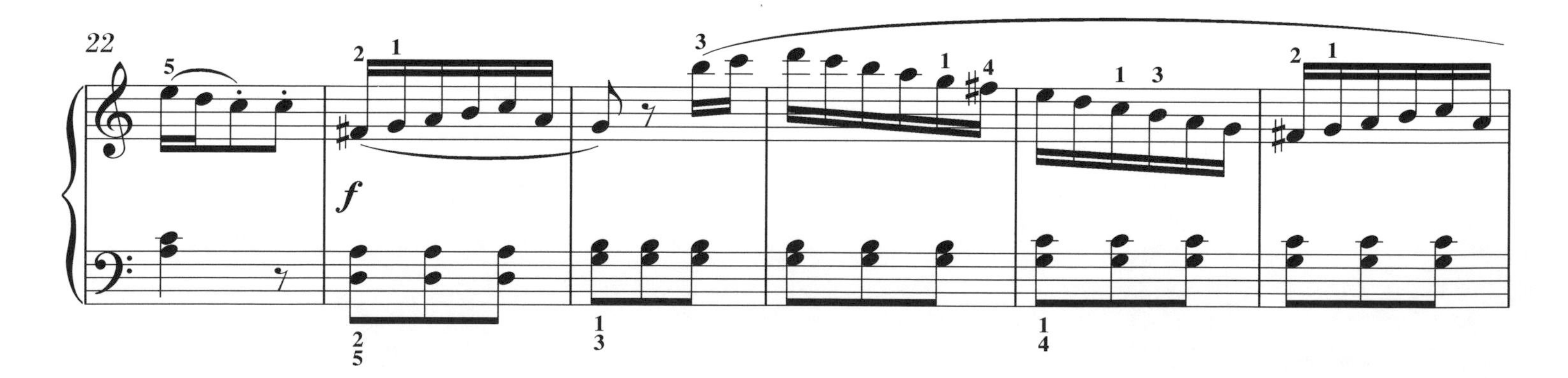

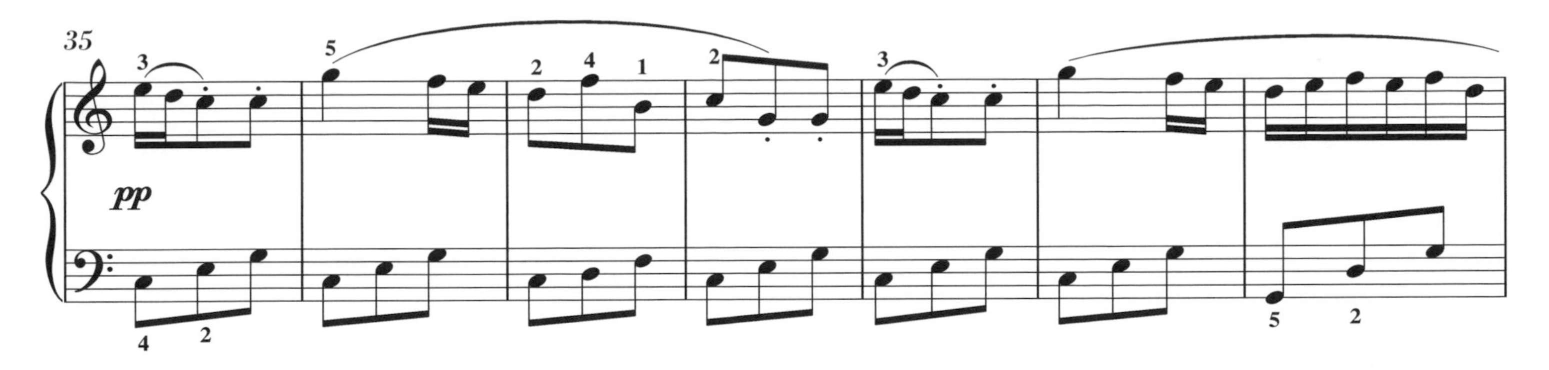
35
pp

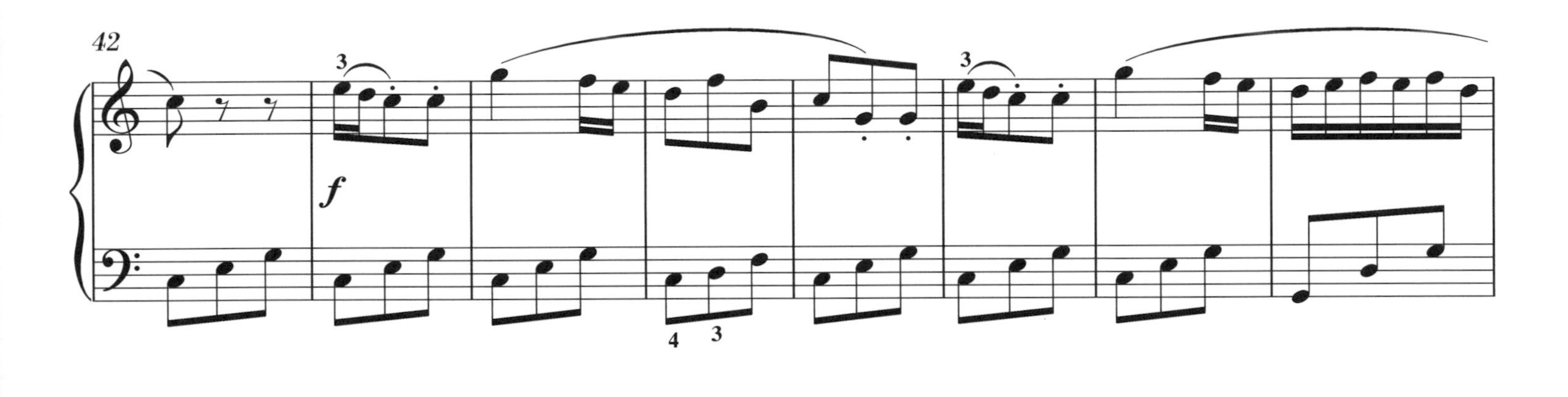
42
f

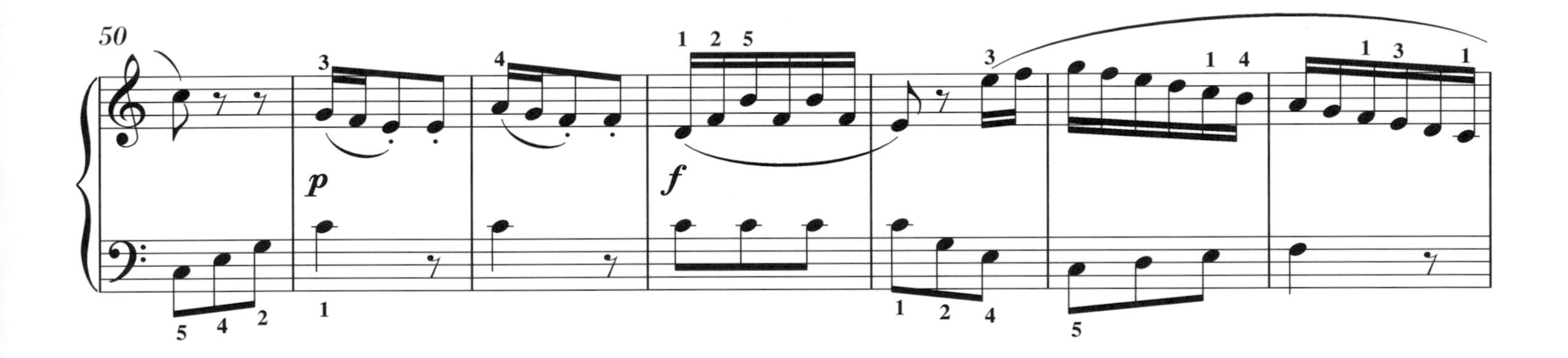
50
p
f

57
p
f

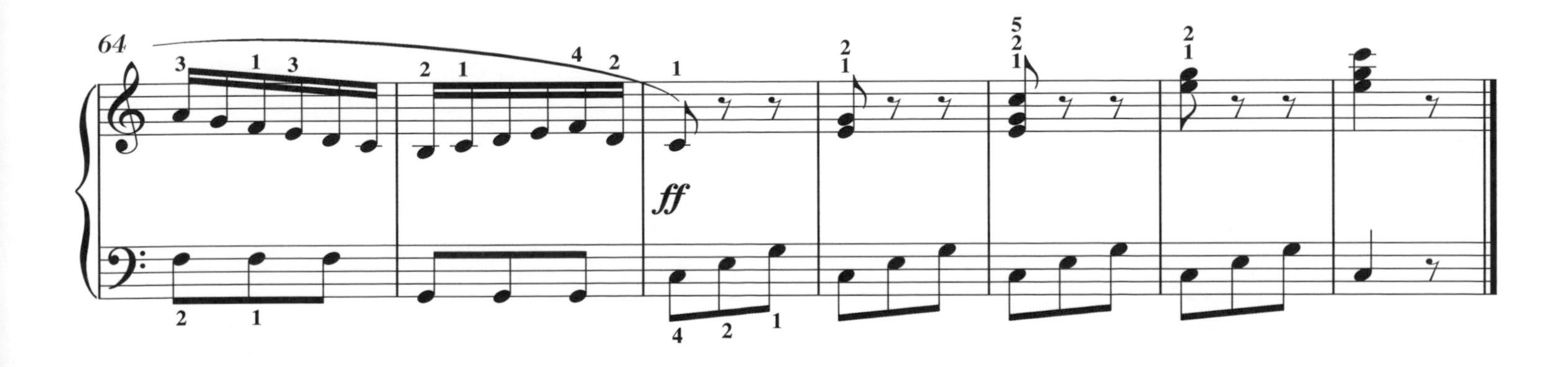
64
ff

LABORUM
DULCE
LENIMEN
G. SCHIRMER

Sonatina in G Major

I

Muzio Clementi
Op. 36, No. 2

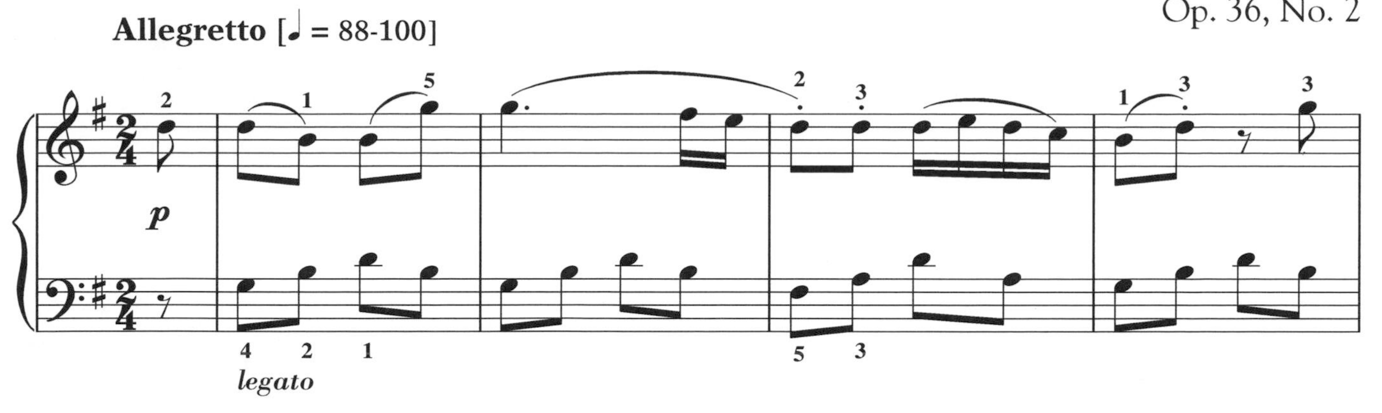

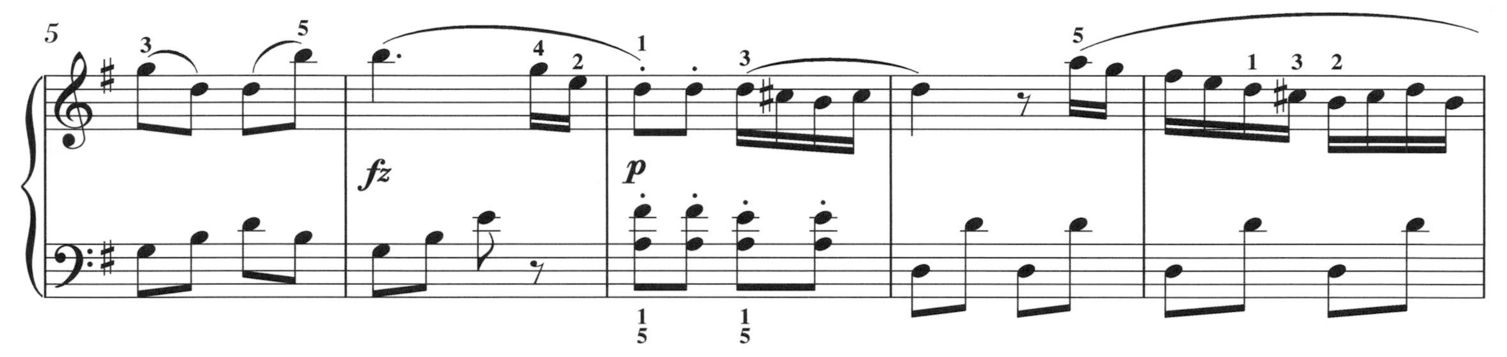

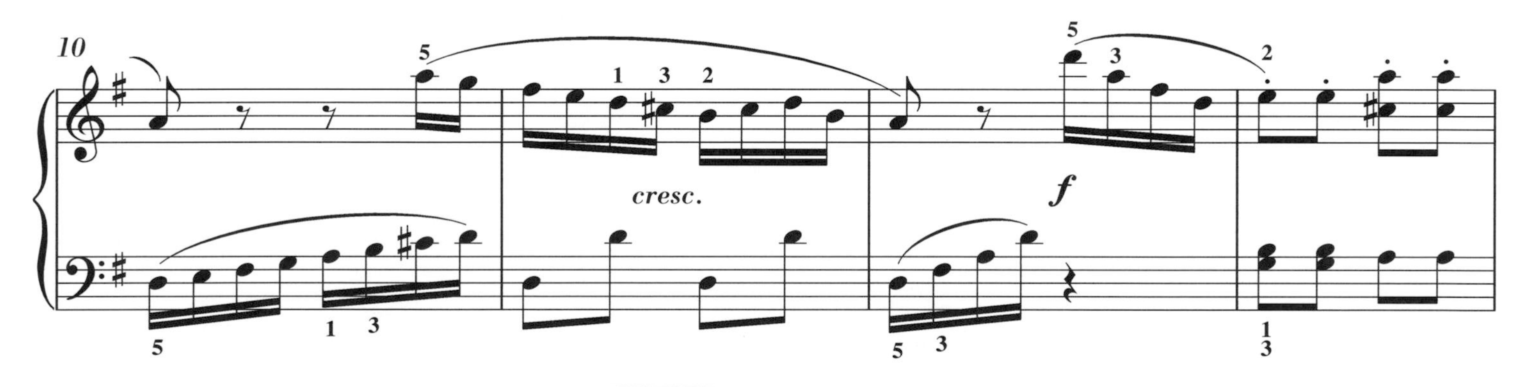

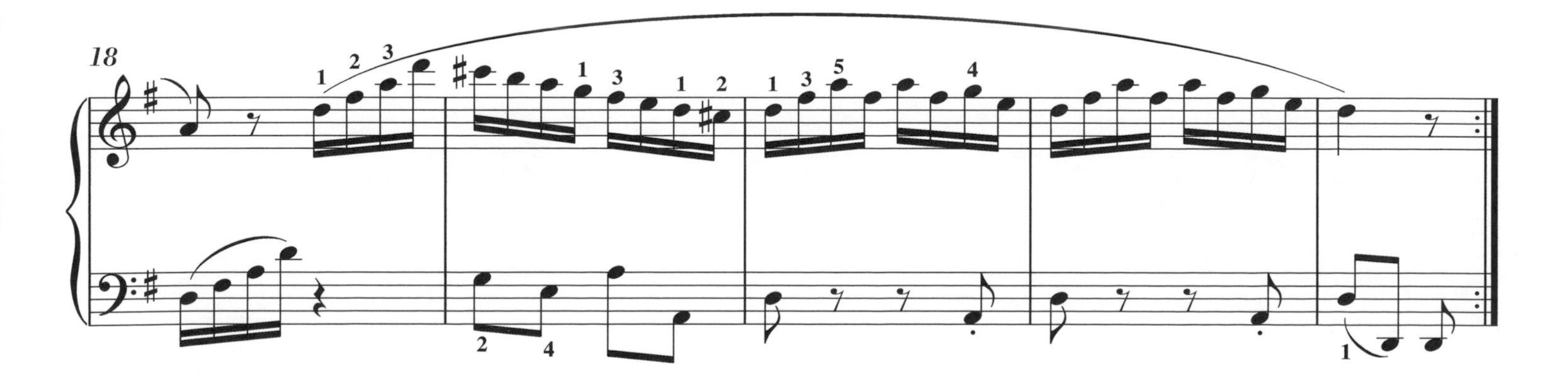

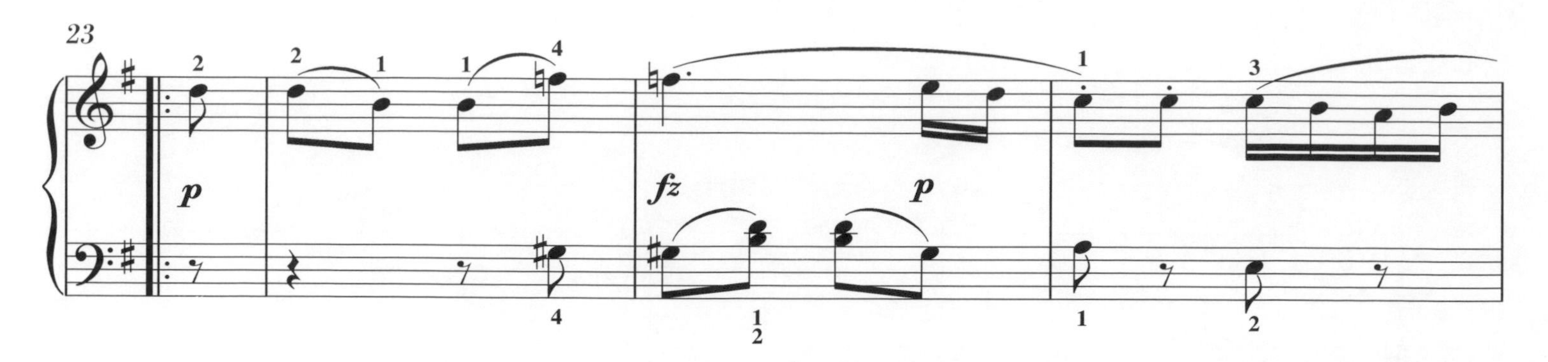
23
p
fz
p

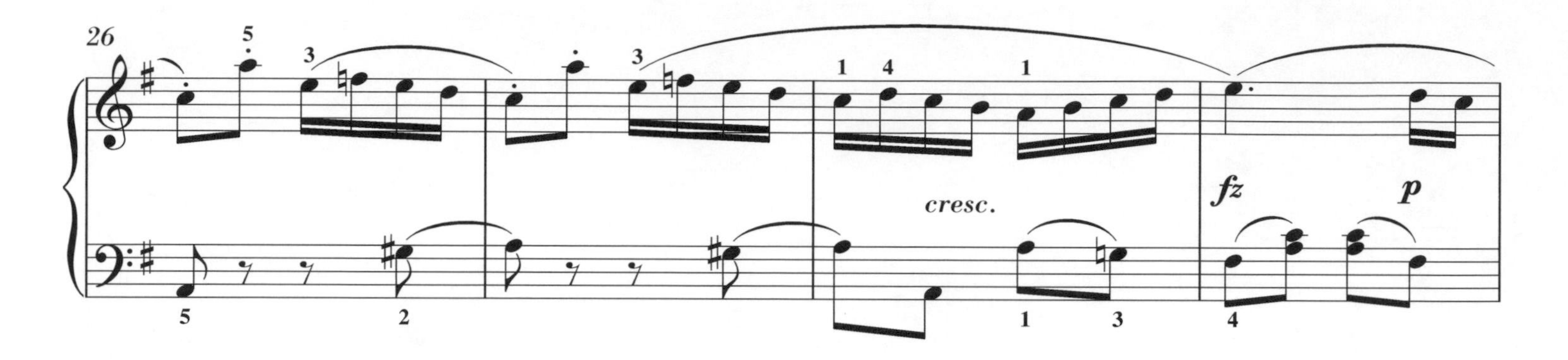
26
cresc.
fz
p

30
f

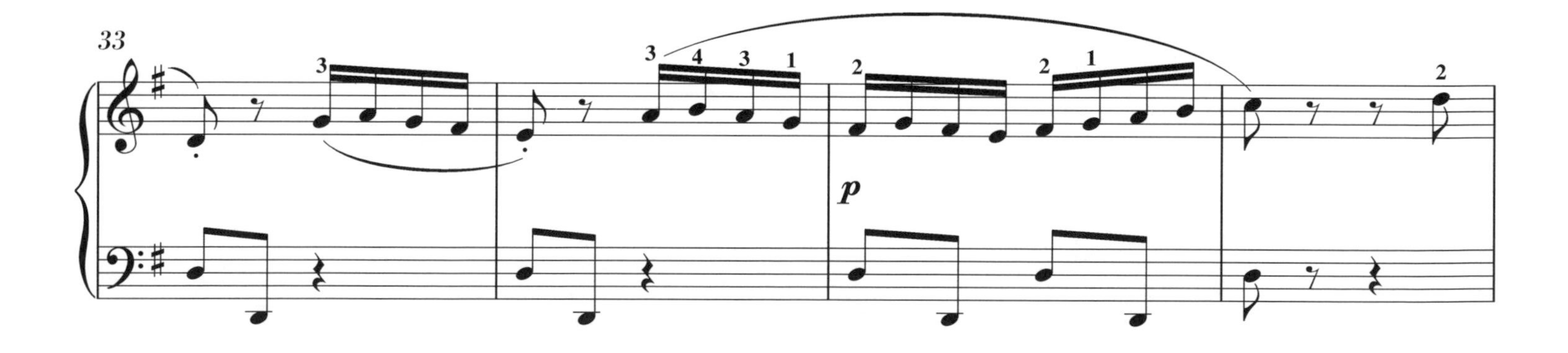
33
p

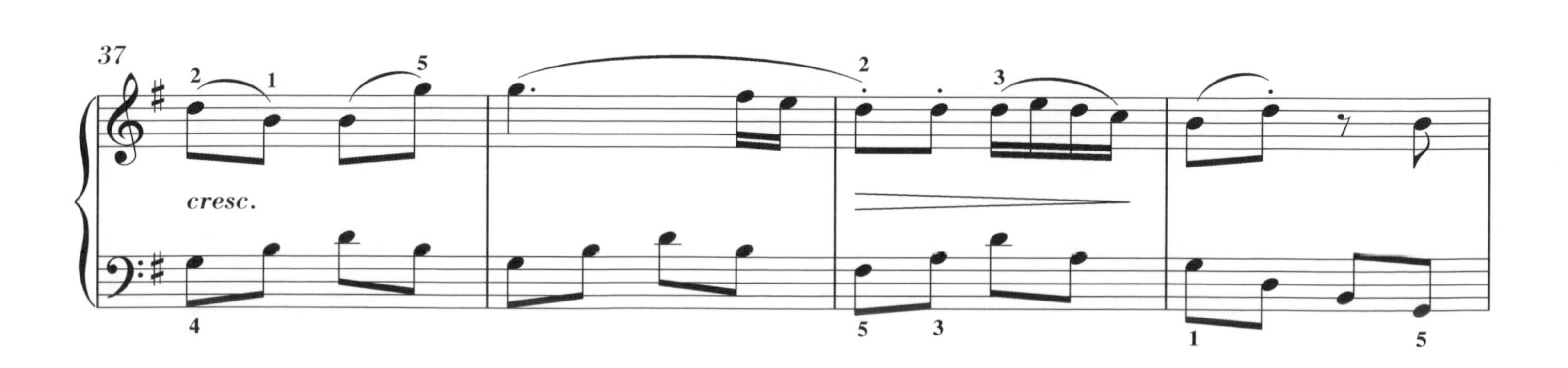
37
cresc.

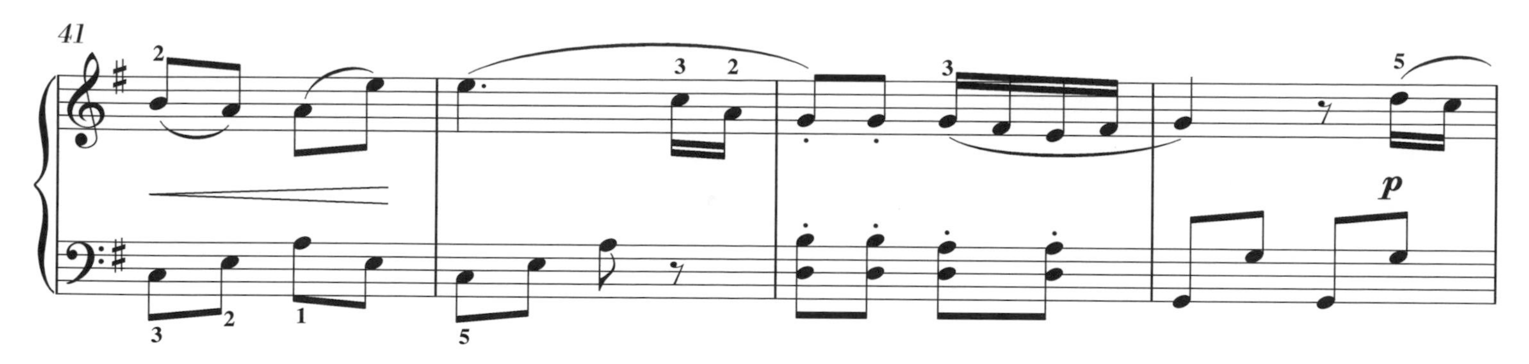
41
p

45
cresc.
f

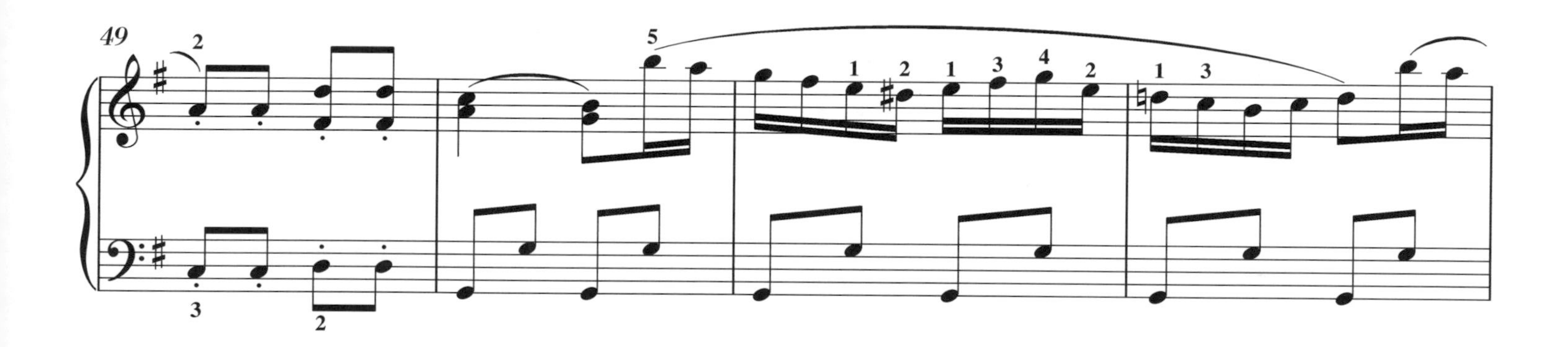
49

53

56

II
Allegretto [♩ = 80-92]

p dolce
legato

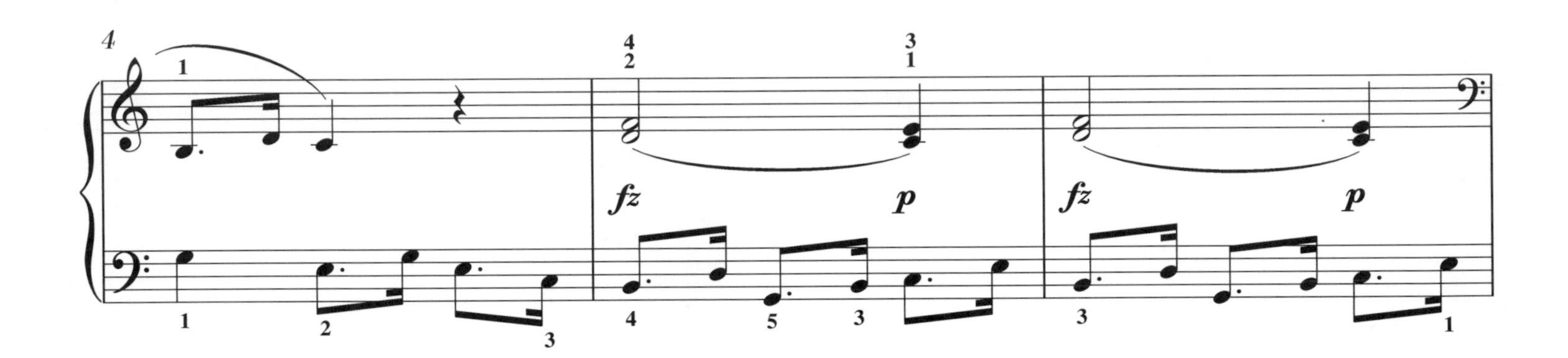
fz
p
fz
p

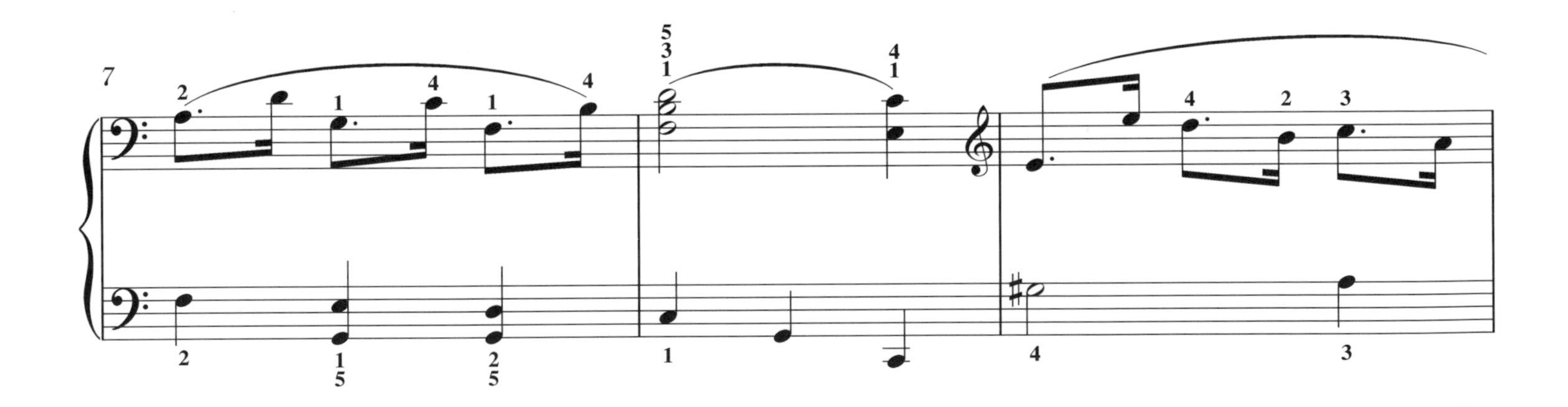

cresc.

13
f

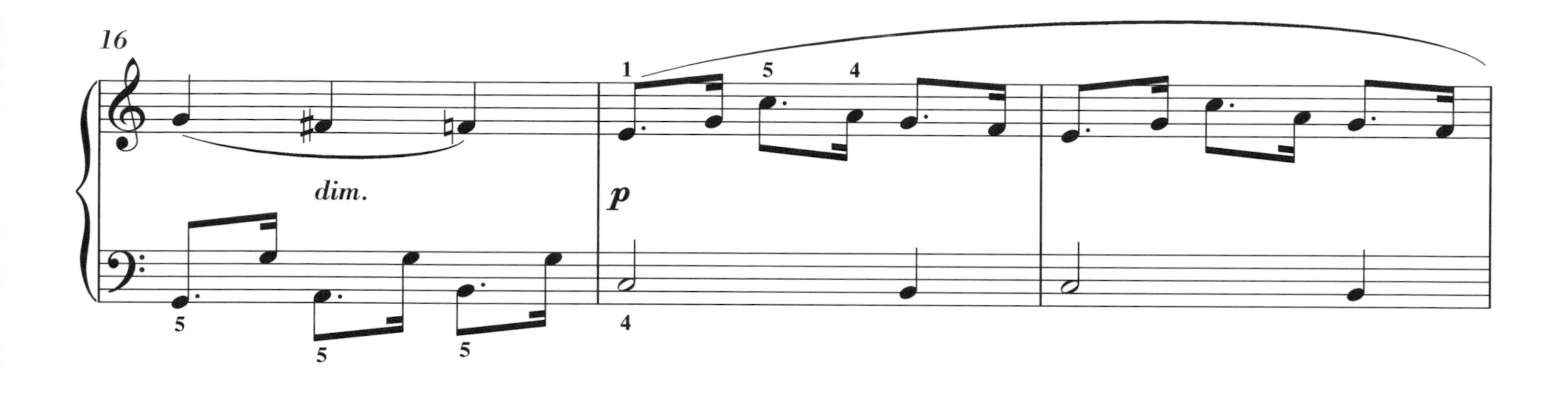
16
dim.
p

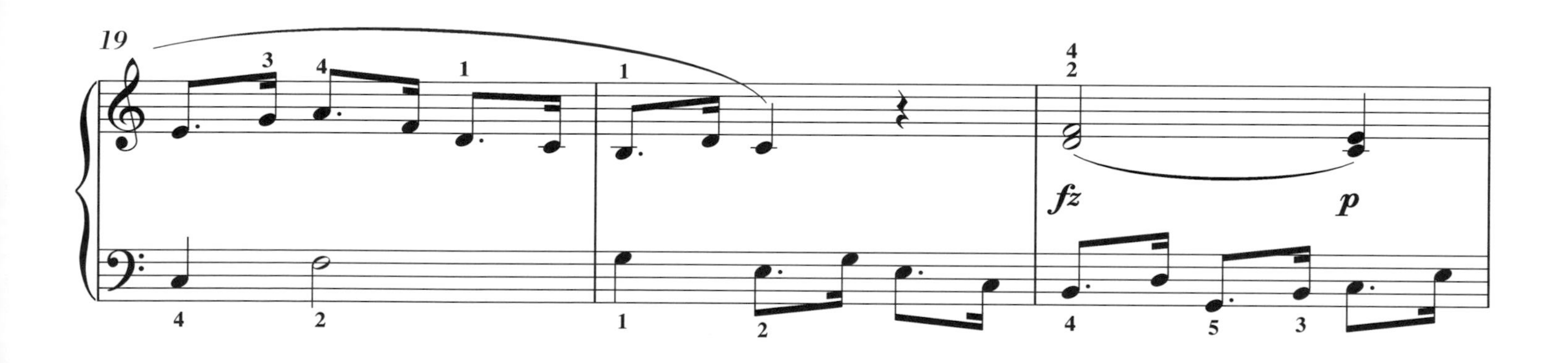
19
fz
p

22
fz
p

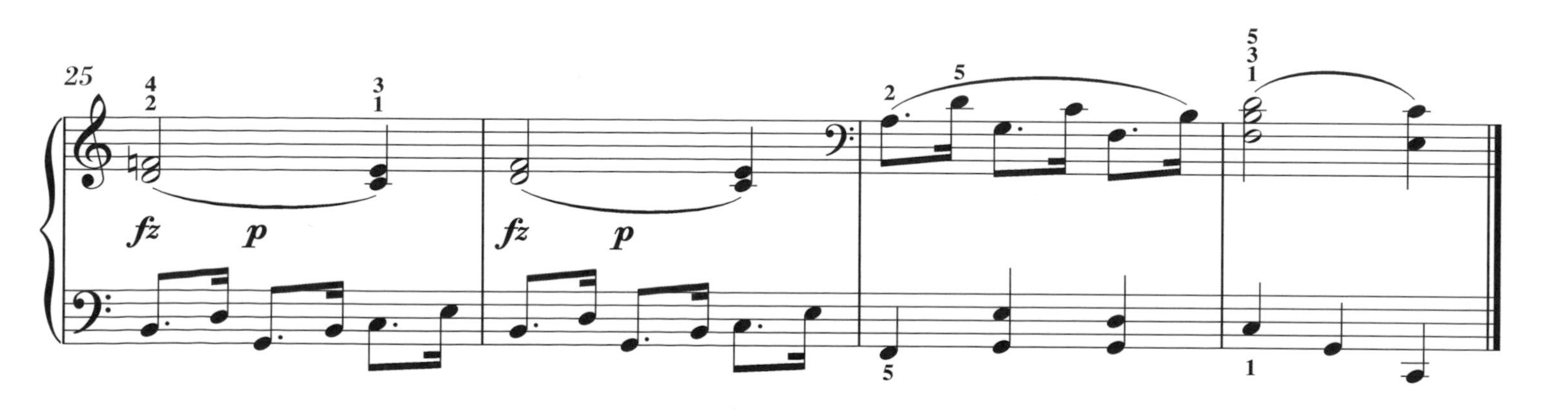
25
fz
p
fz
p

III

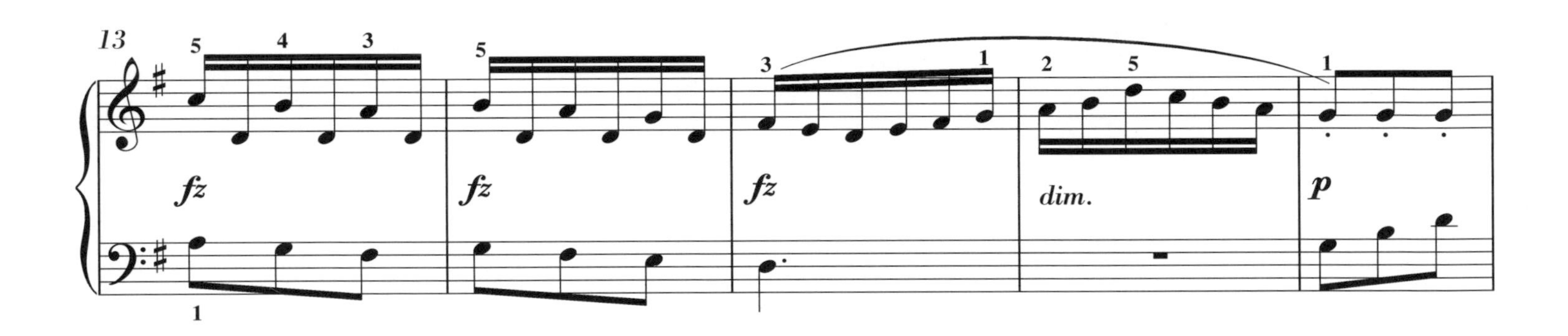

30
fz
fz

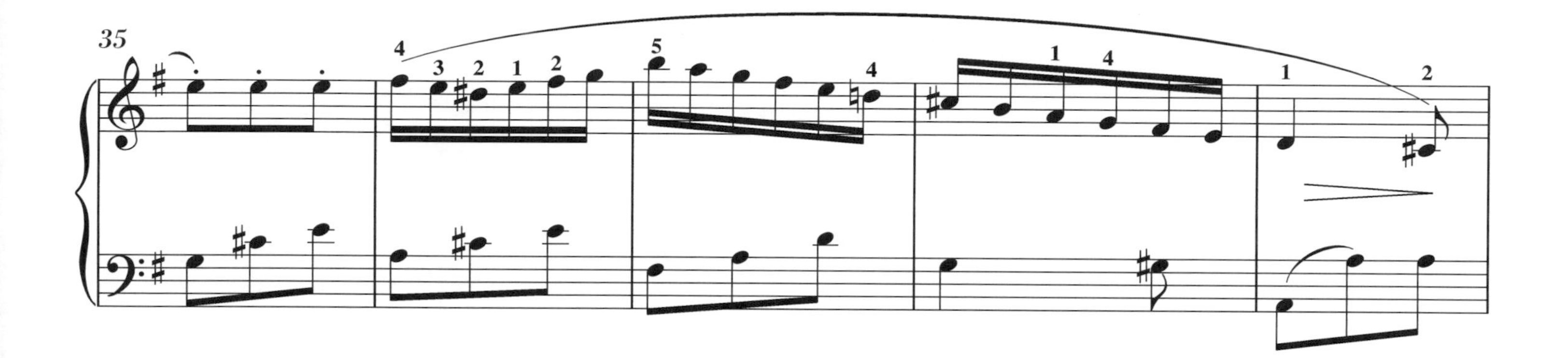
35

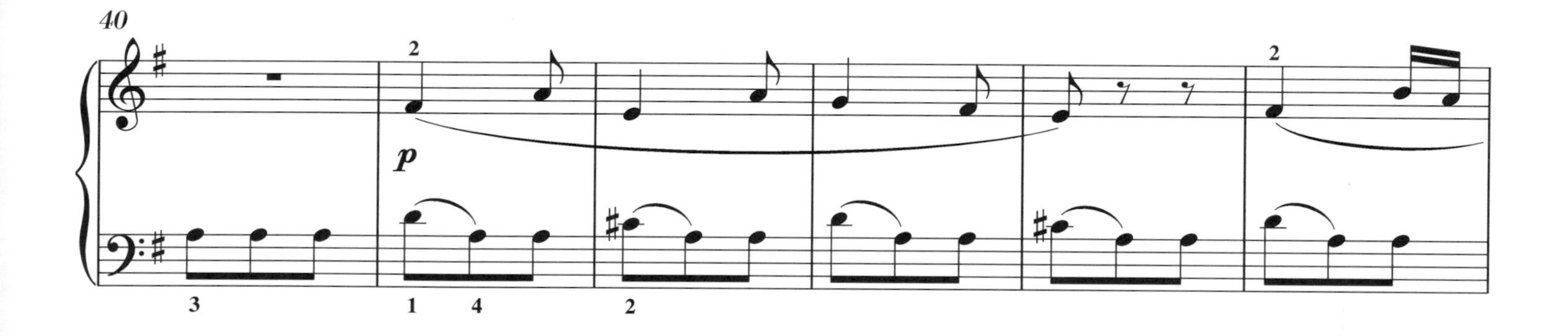
40
p

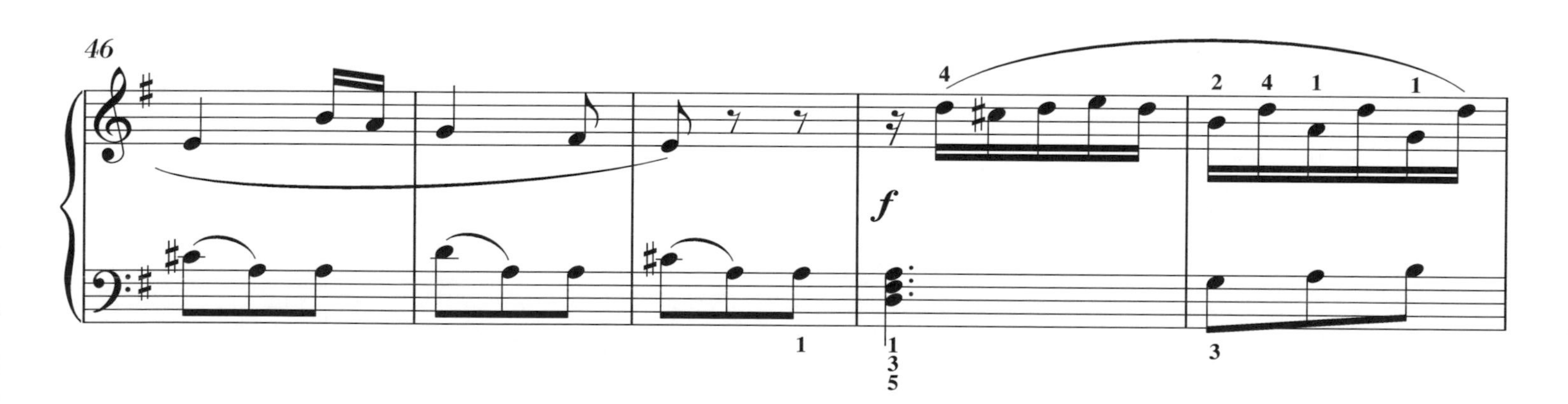
46
f

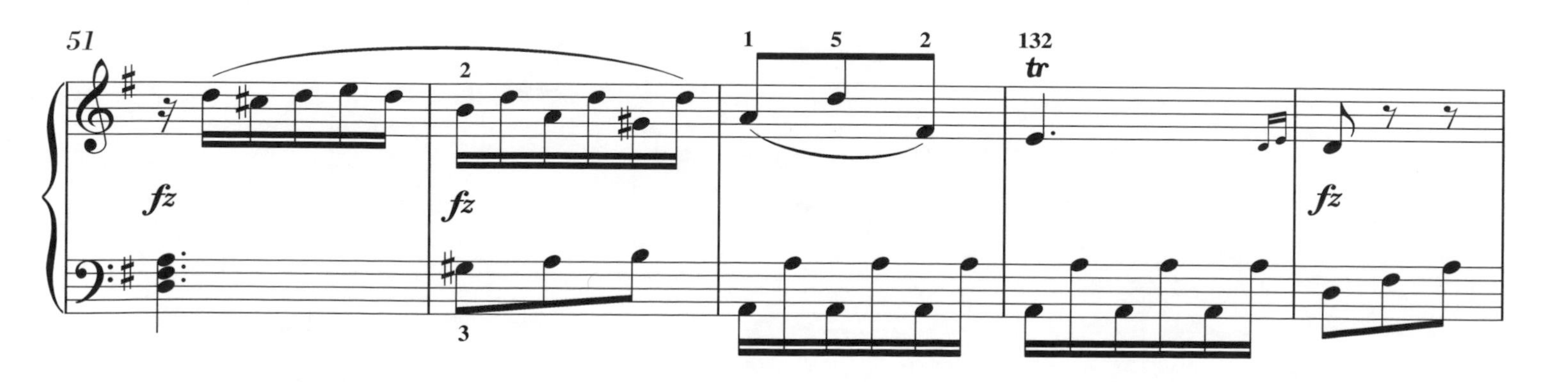
51
fz
fz
tr
fz

56
dim.
p

62
f

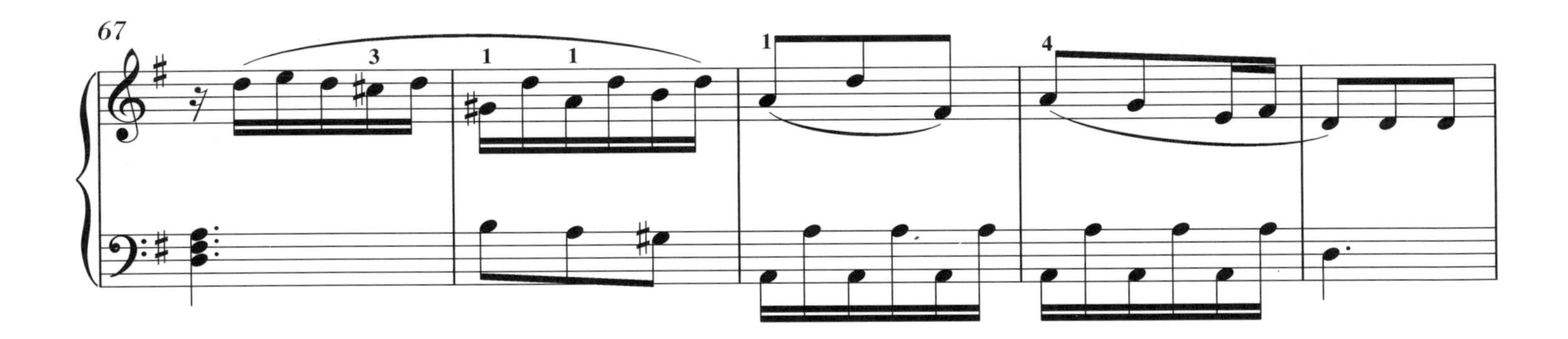
67

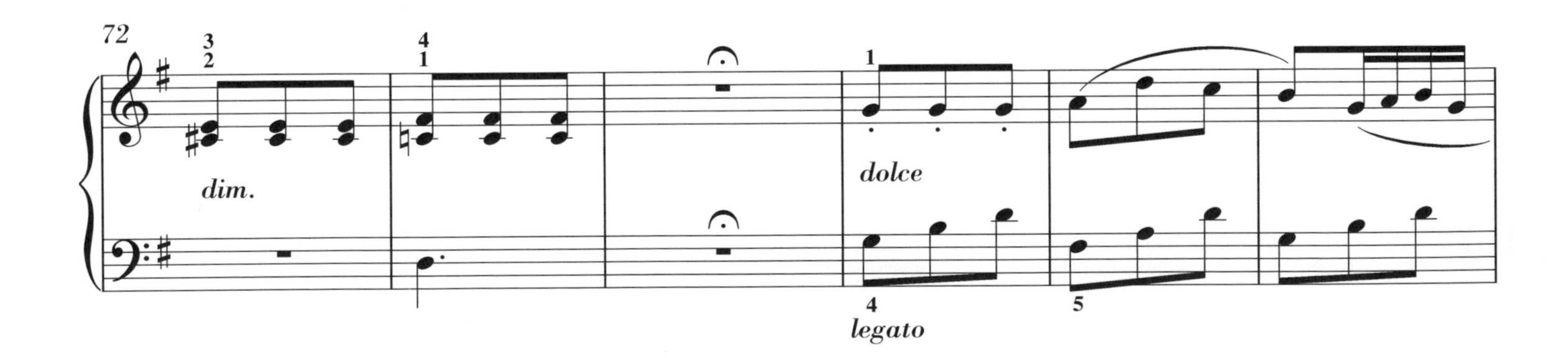
72
dim.
dolce
legato

78
f

83
fz

88
fz
fz
dim.
p

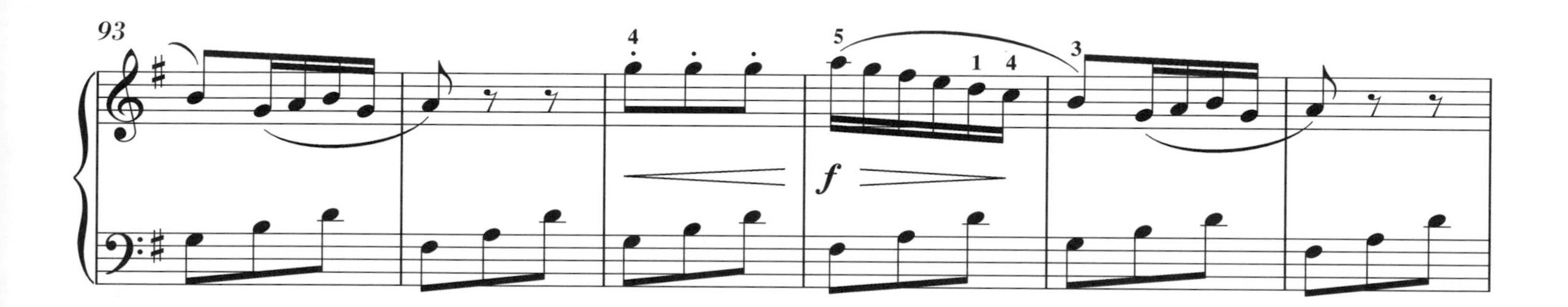
93
f

99
cresc.
f
dim.

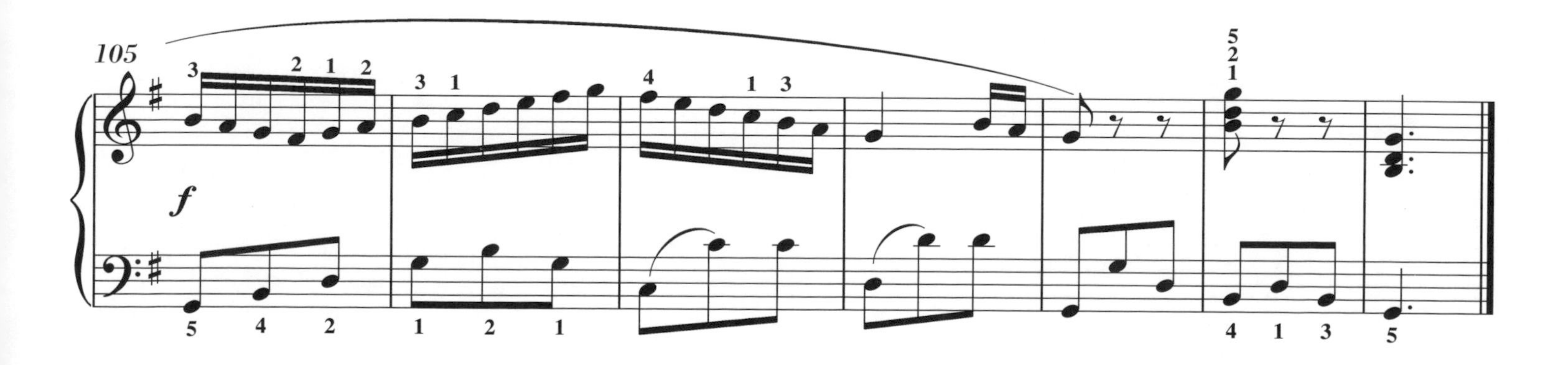
105
f

Sonatina in C Major

I

Muzio Clementi
Op. 36, No. 3

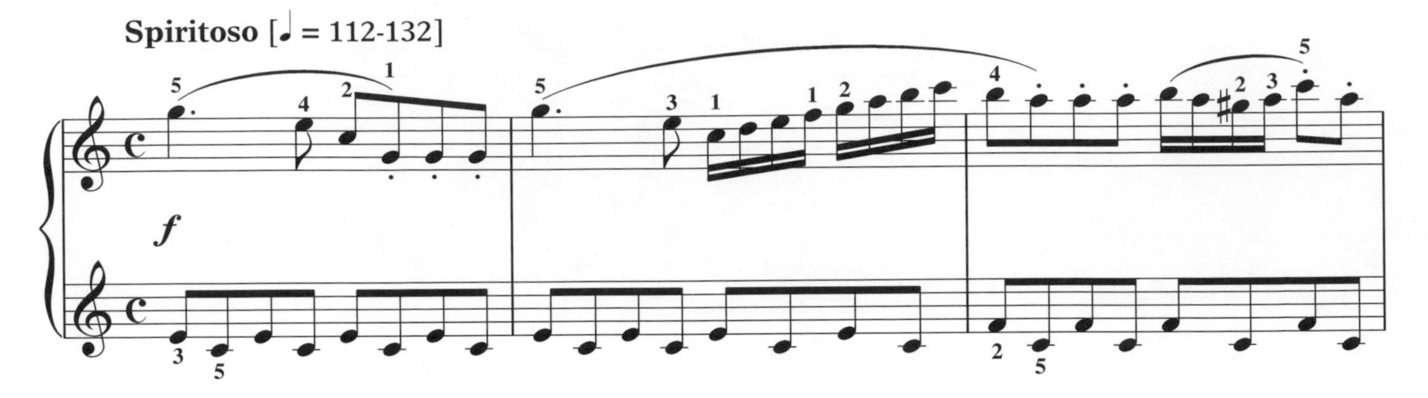

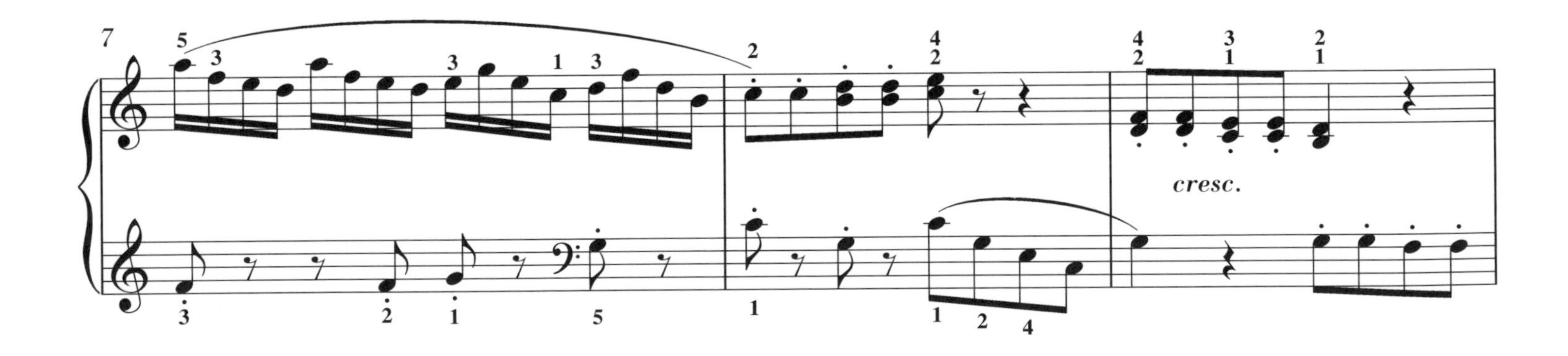

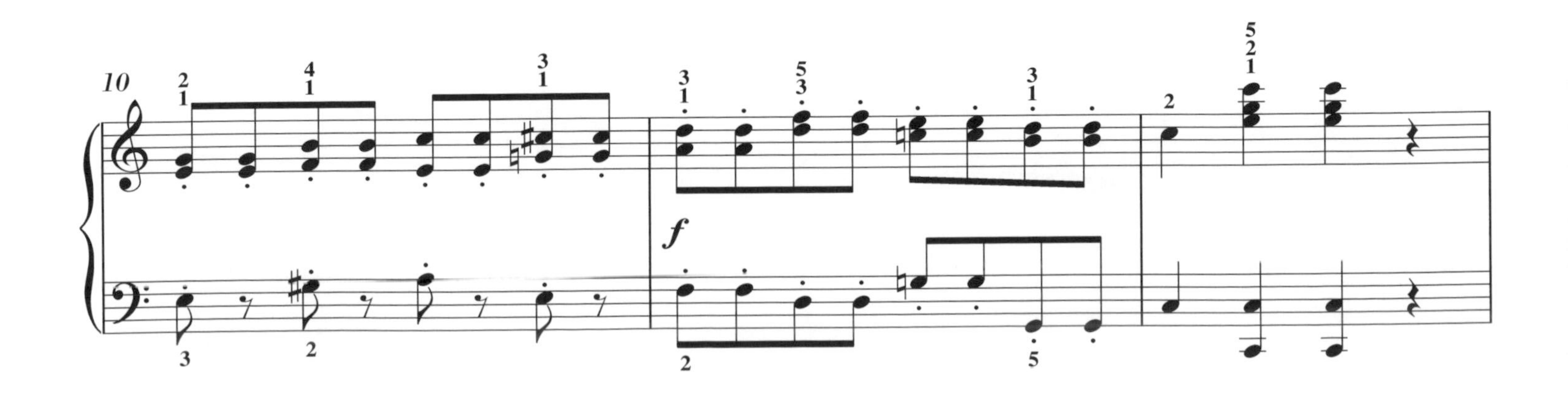

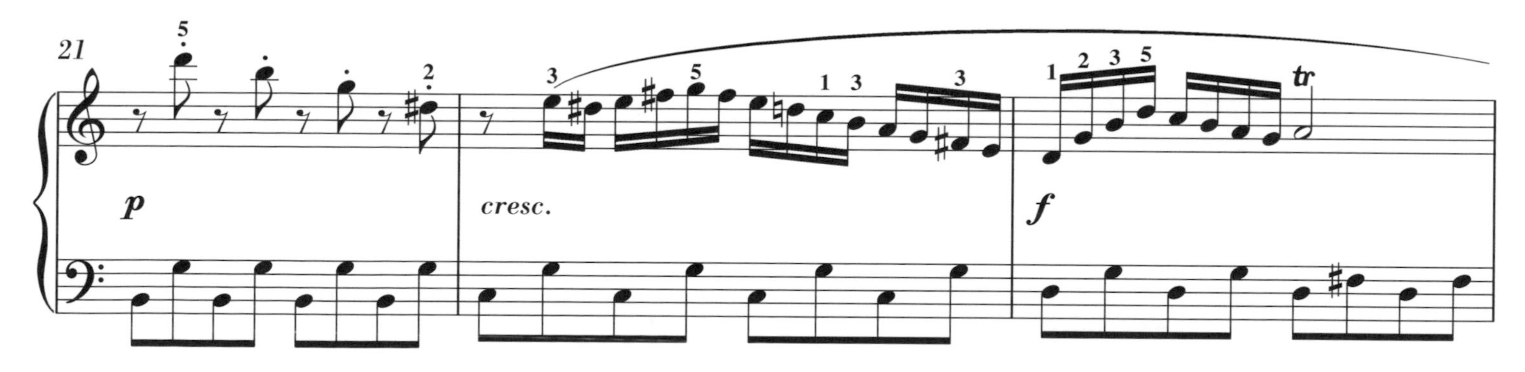

* optional

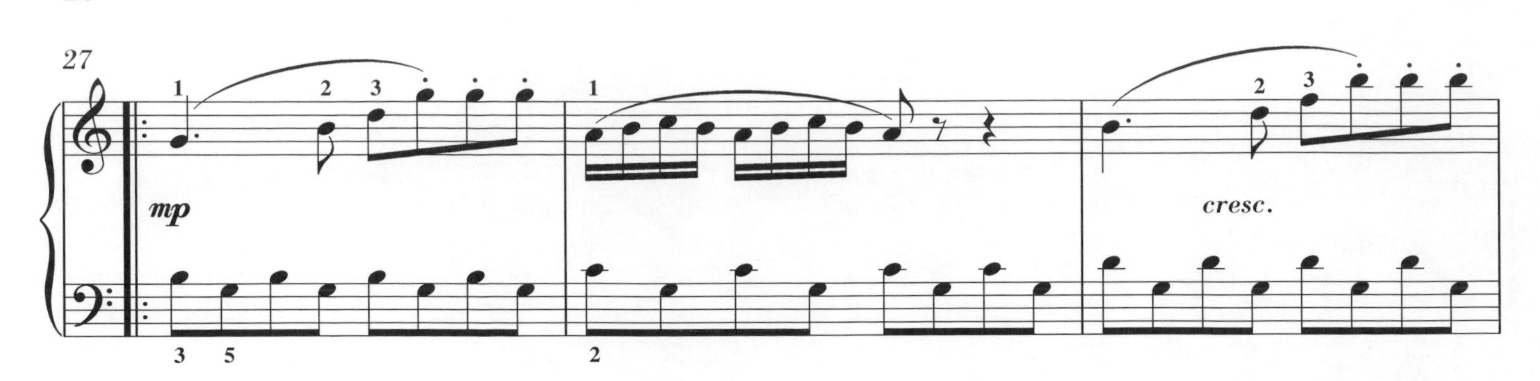
27
mp
cresc.

30
f
ff

32
dim.

34
p
pp
f

37

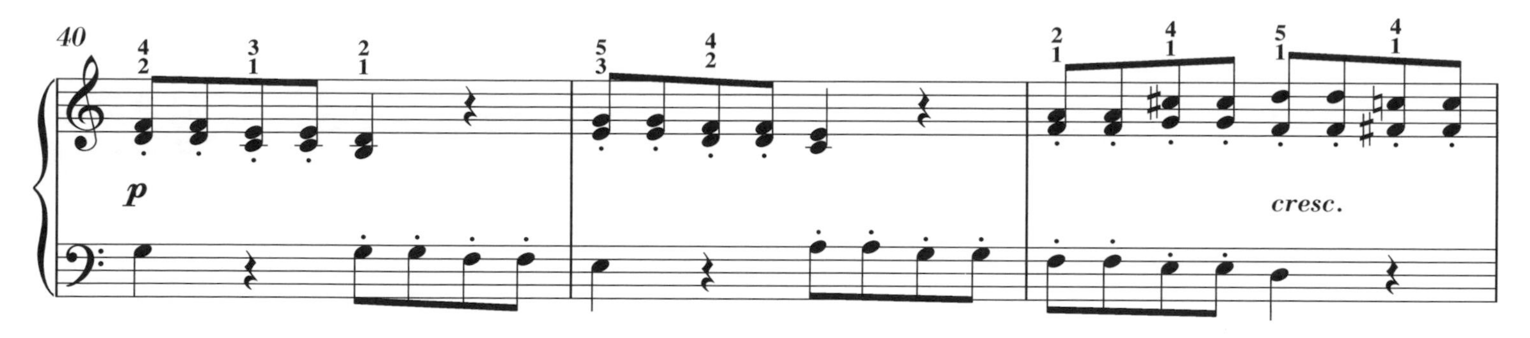
40
p
cresc.

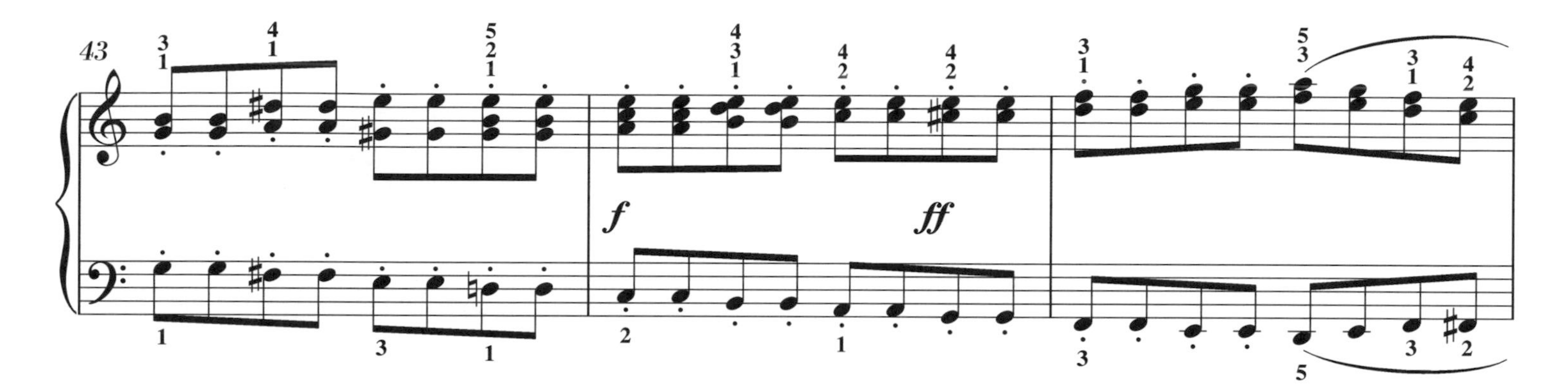
43
f
ff

46

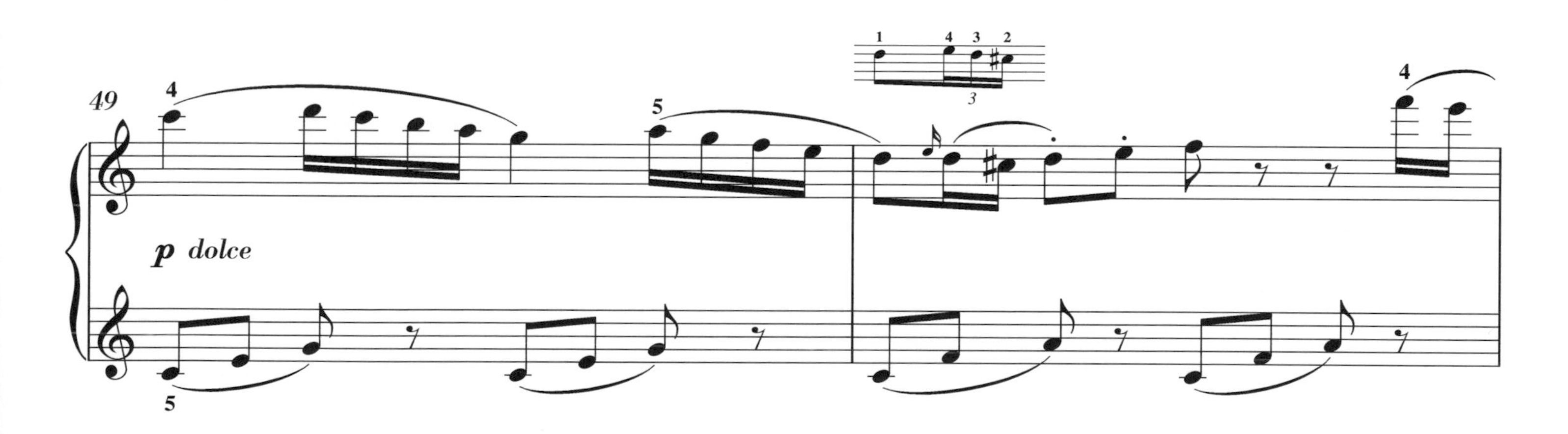
49
p dolce

51

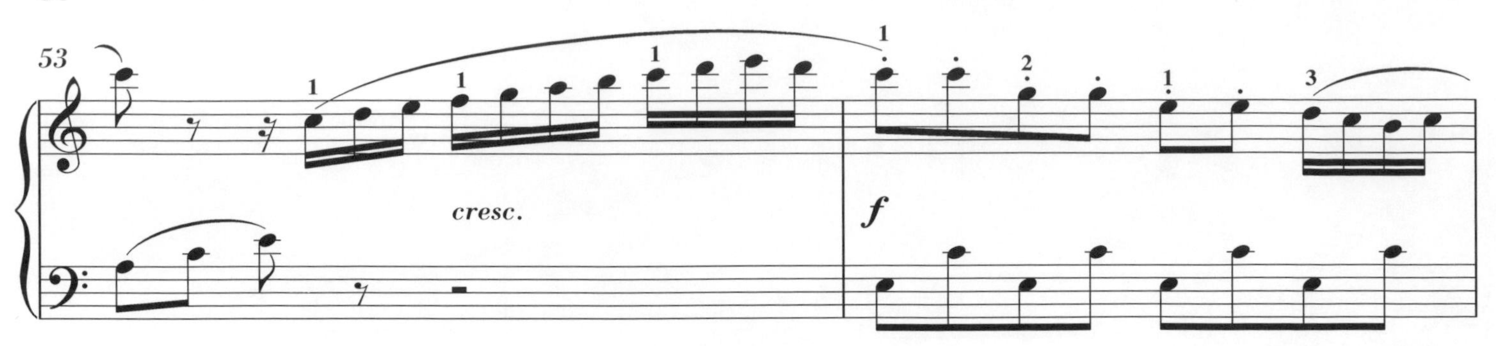
53
cresc.
f

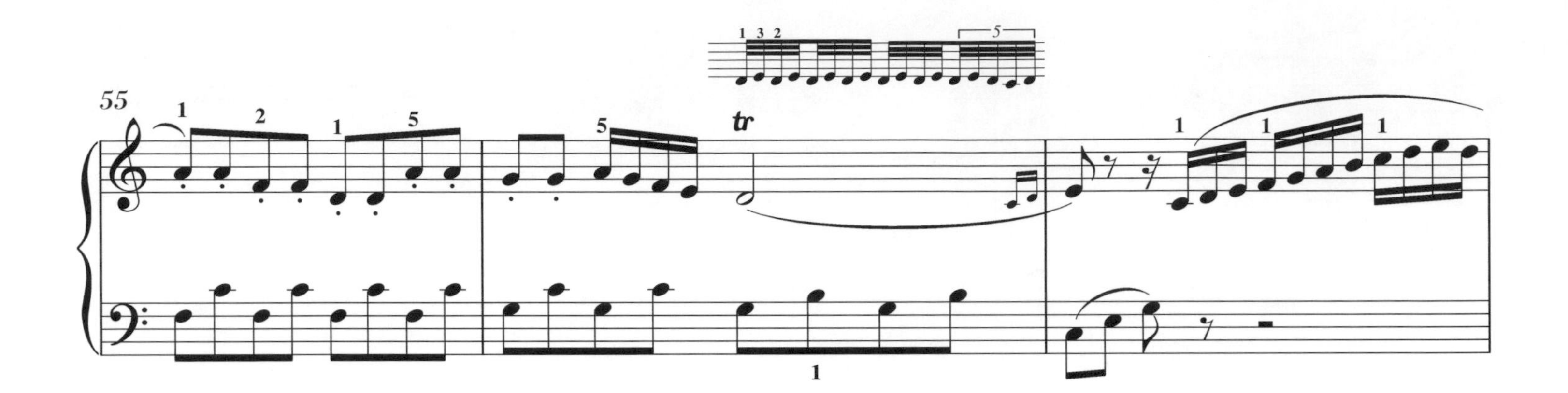
55
tr

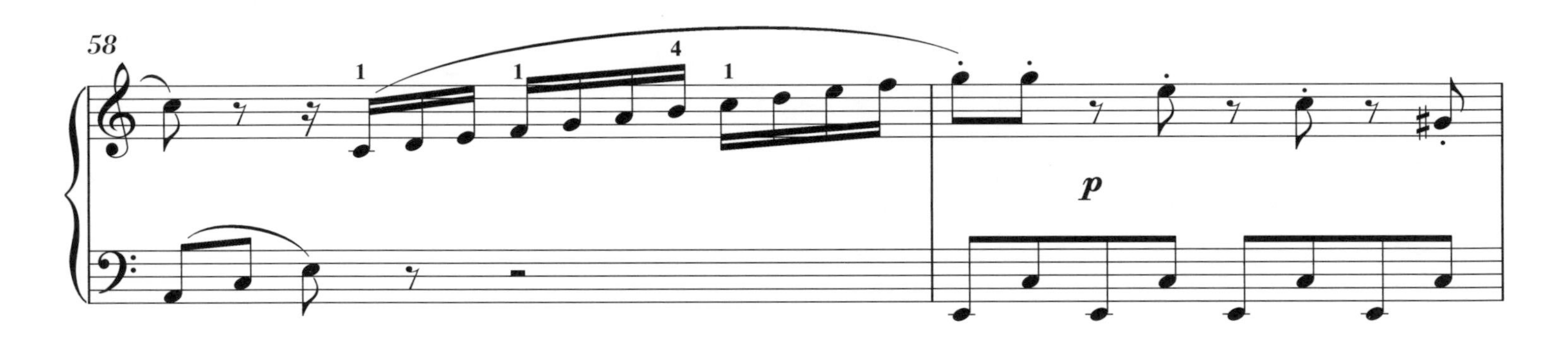
58
p

60
cresc.
f
tr

62
p
cresc.
f

II

Un poco adagio [♩ = 72-88]

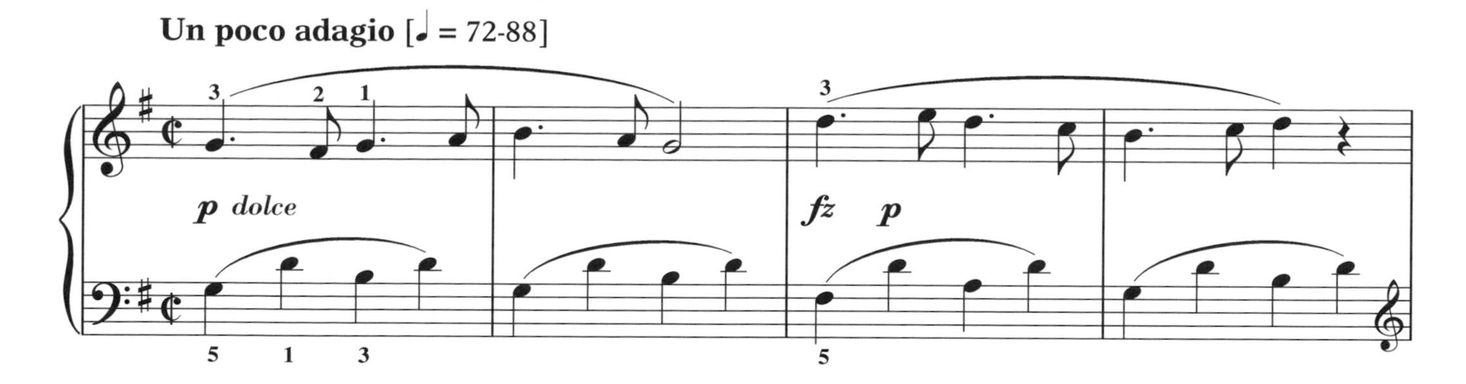

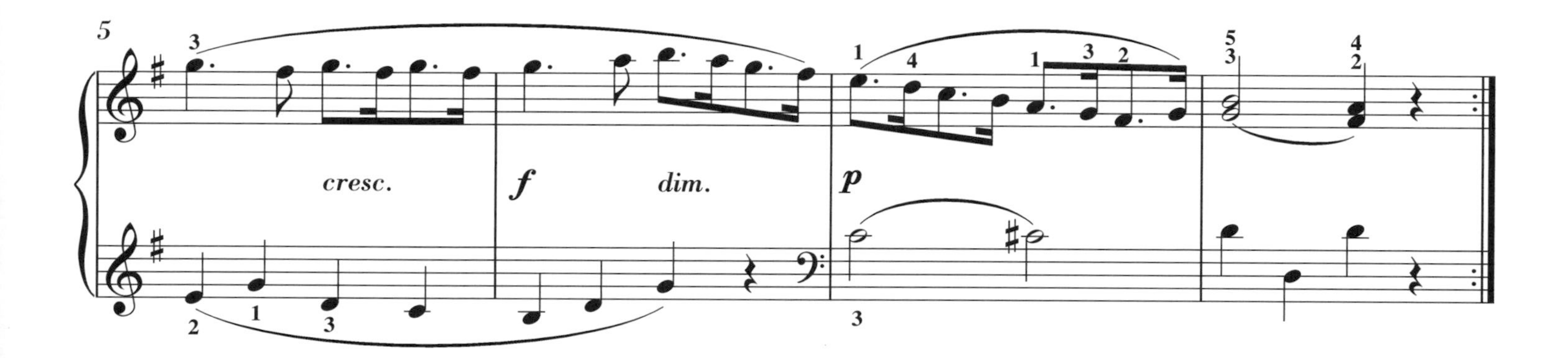

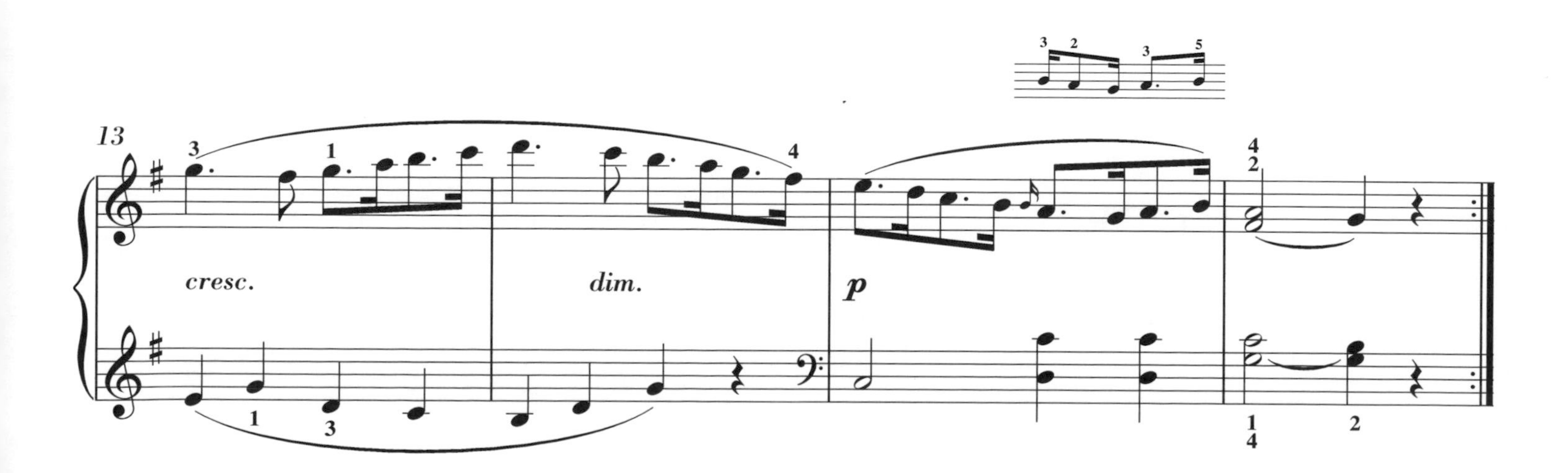

III

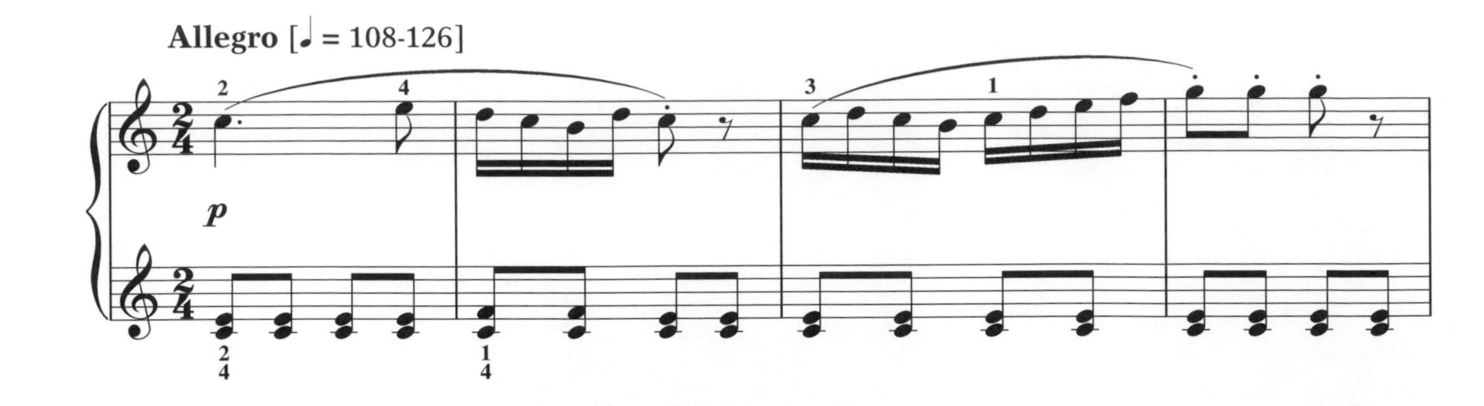

22
fz
fz

26
p
f

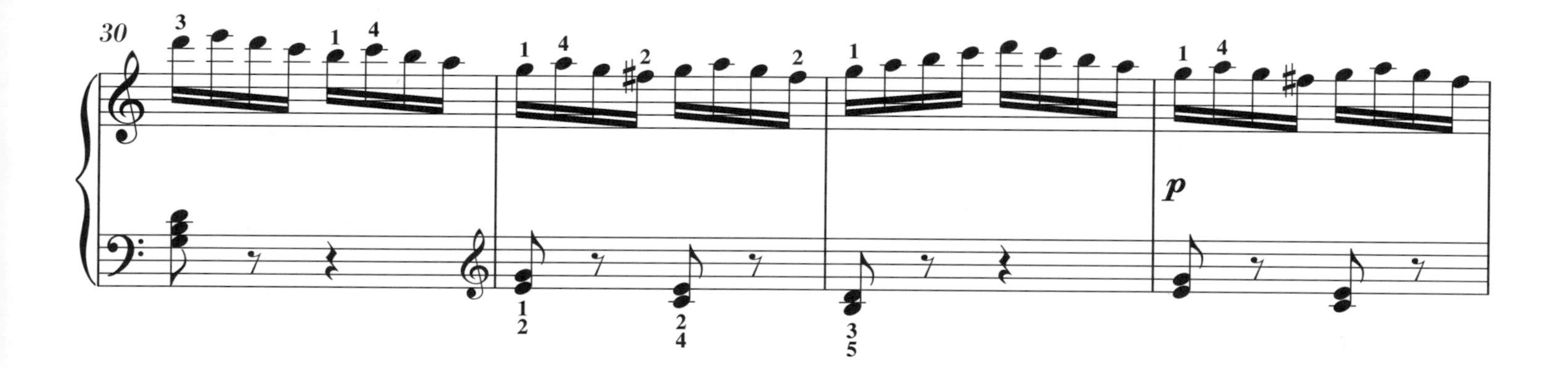
30
p

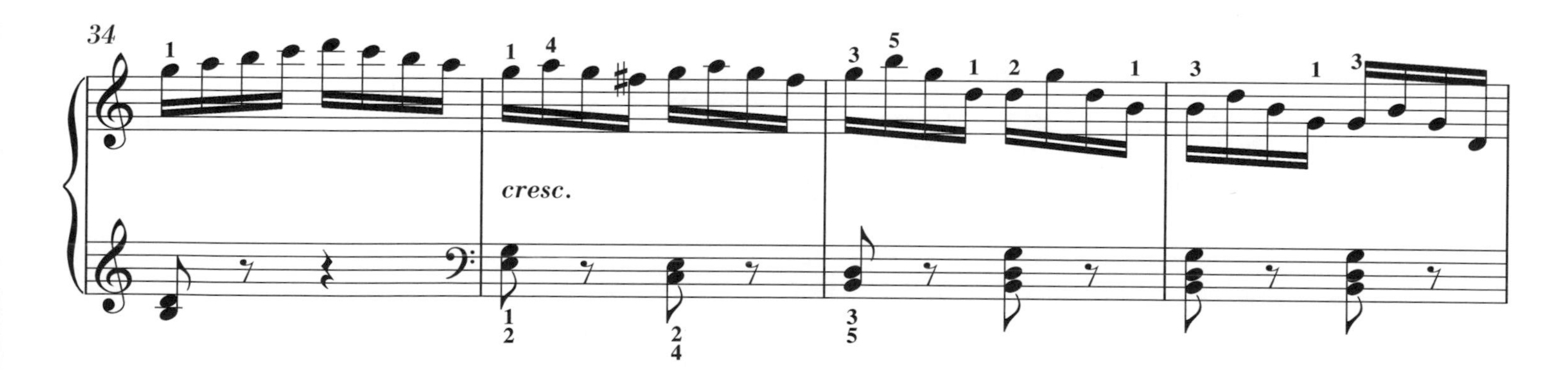
34
cresc.

38
dim.
p

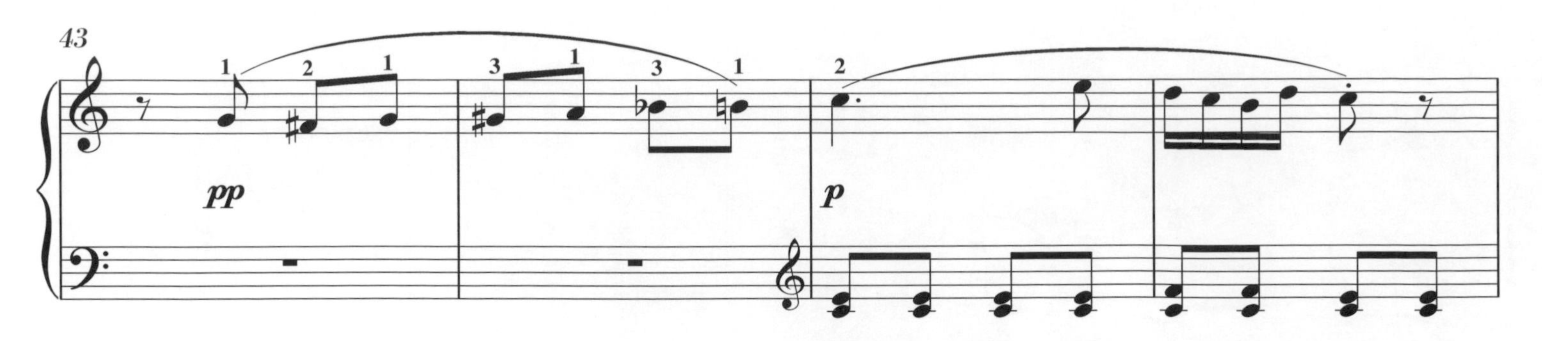
43
1
2
1
3
1
3
1
2
pp
p

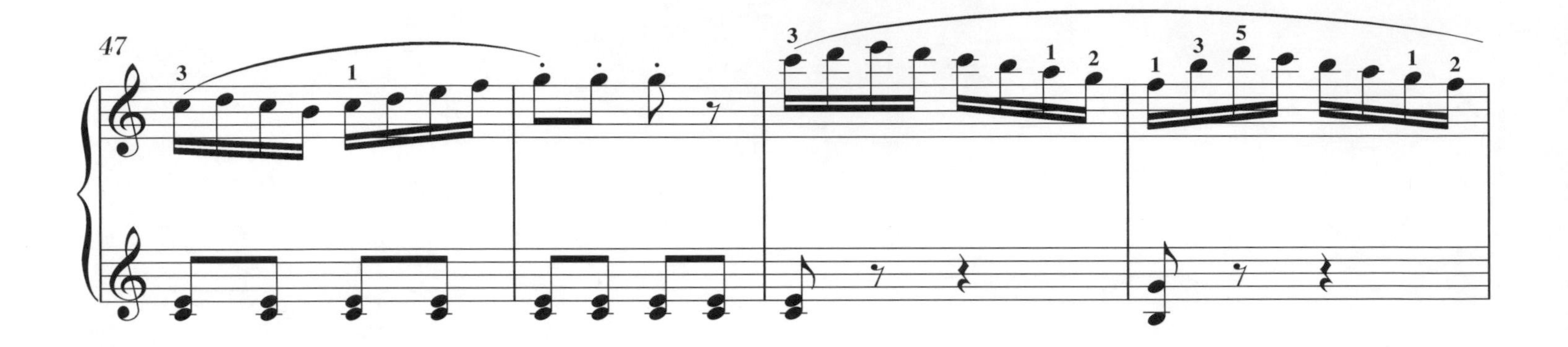
47
3
1
3
1
2
1
3
5
1
2

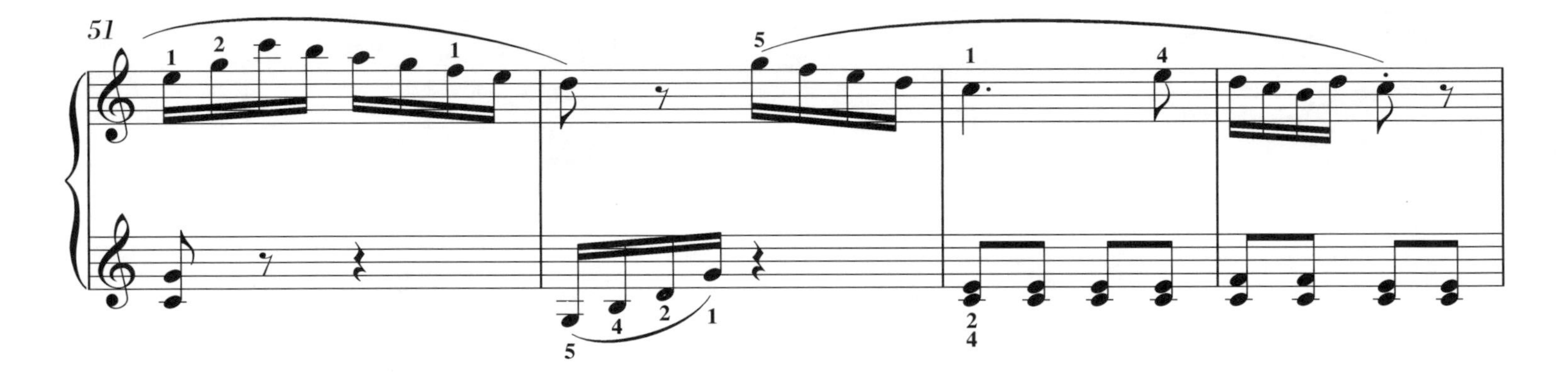
51
1
2
1
5
1
4
5
4
2
1
2
4

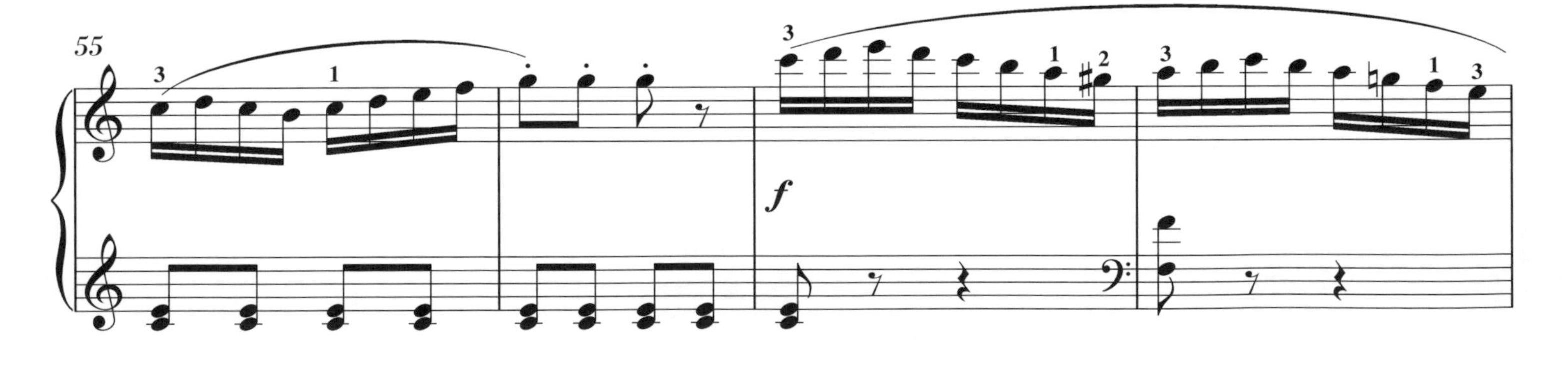
55
3
1
3
1
2
3
1
3
f

59
2
1
4
1
3
3
1
2
fz
p
5

63

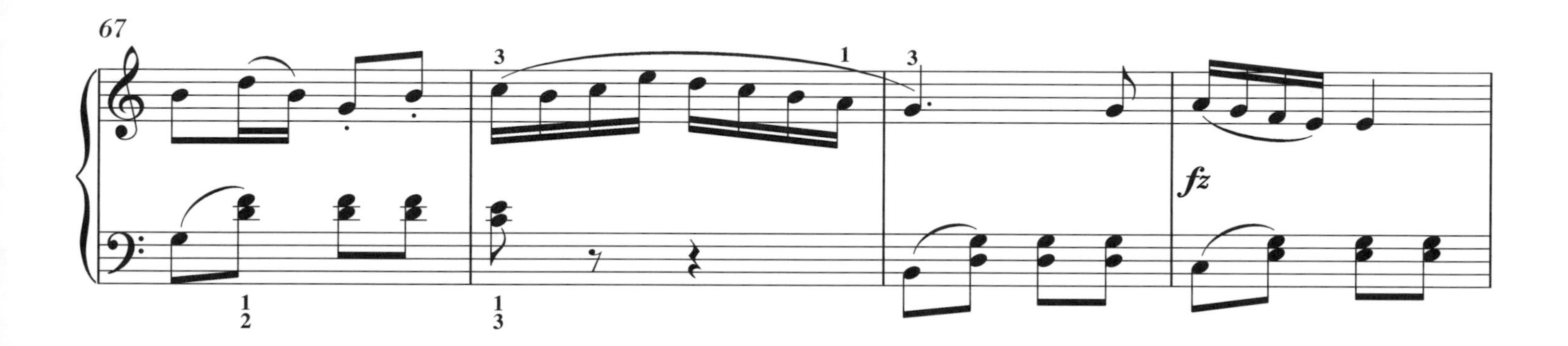
67
3
1
3
fz
1
2
1
3

71
1
1
4
4

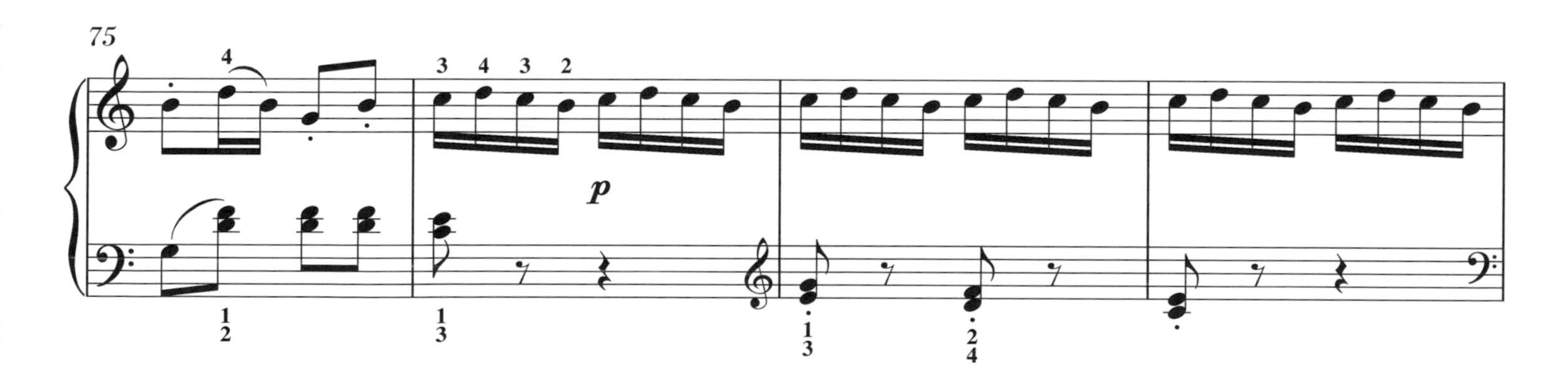
75
4
3 4 3 2
p
1
2
1
3
1
3
2
4

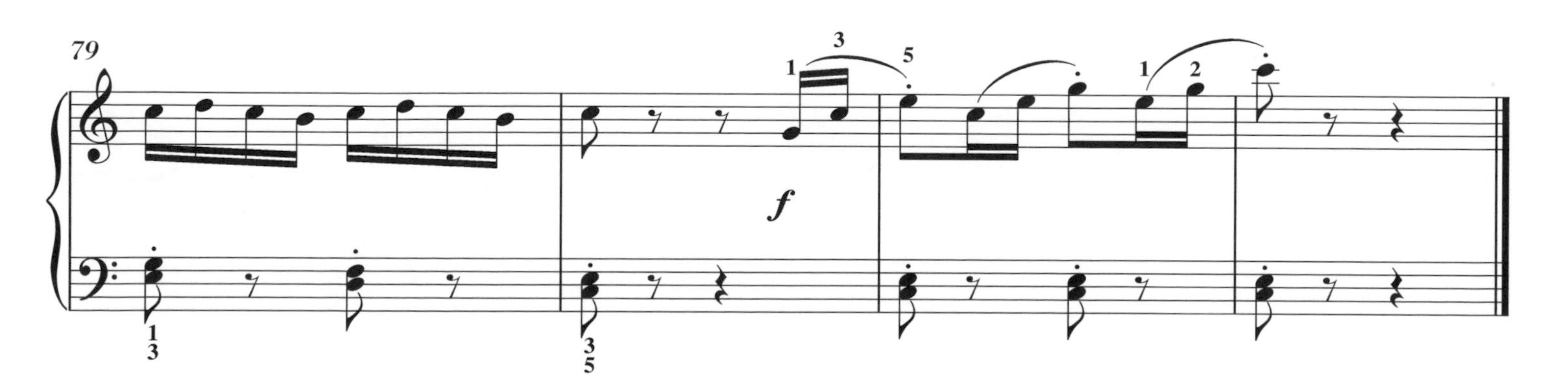
79
1
3
5
1
2
f
1
3
3
5

Sonatina in F Major

I

Muzio Clementi
Op. 36, No. 4

19
fz
fz

23
p dolce
fz
fz

27
cresc.
f

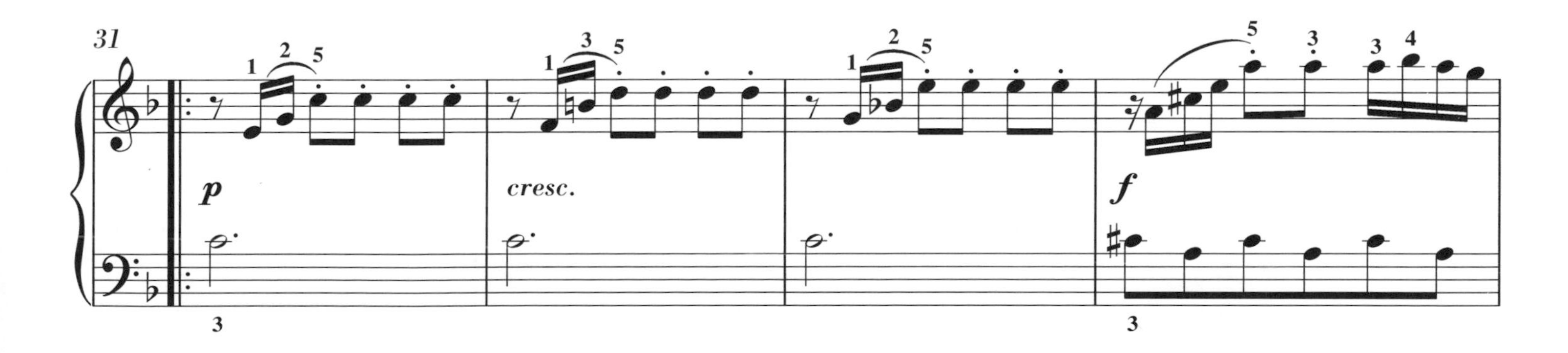
31
p
cresc.
f

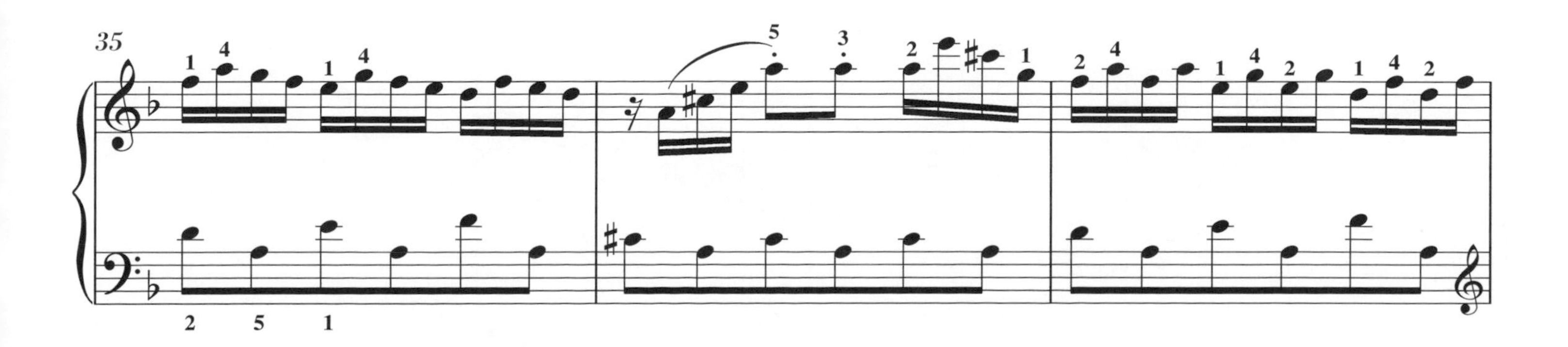
35

38
p

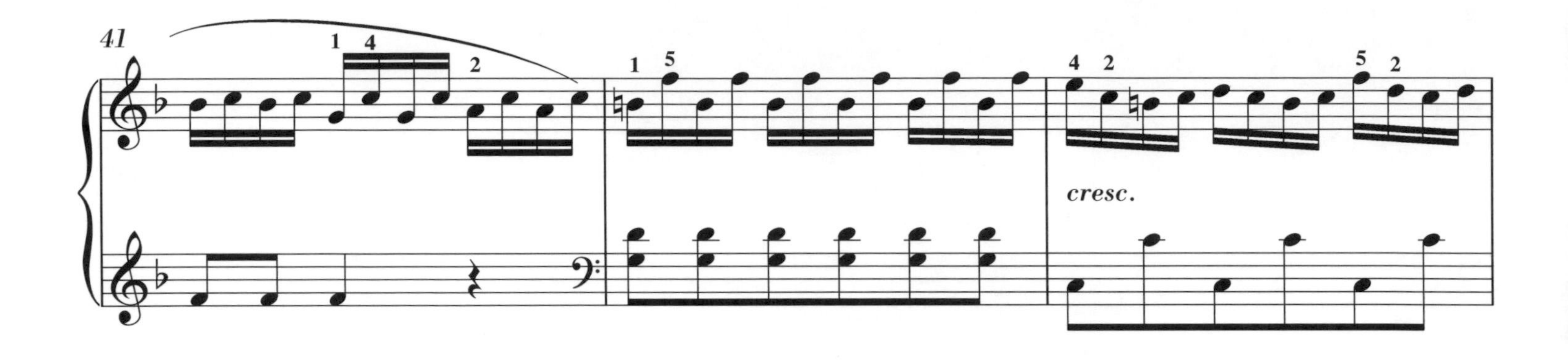
41
cresc.

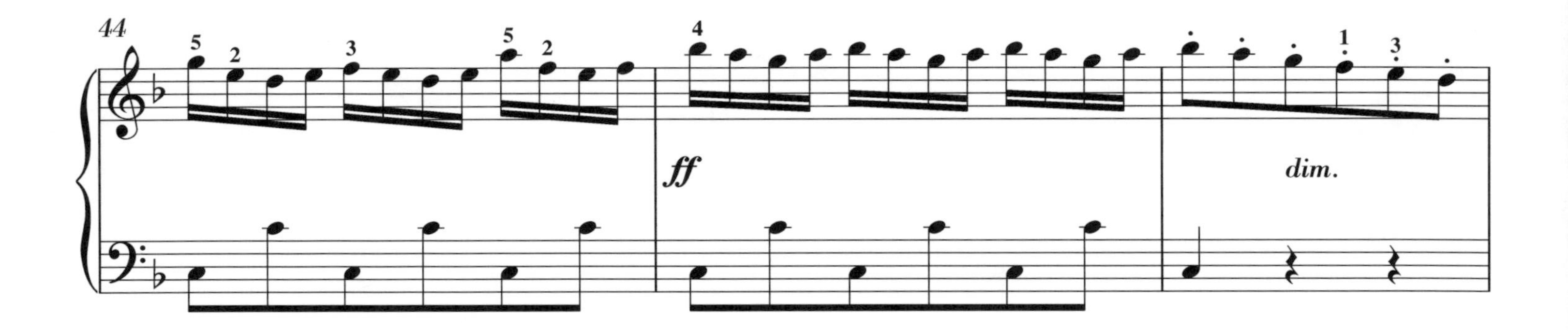
44
ff
dim.

47
p

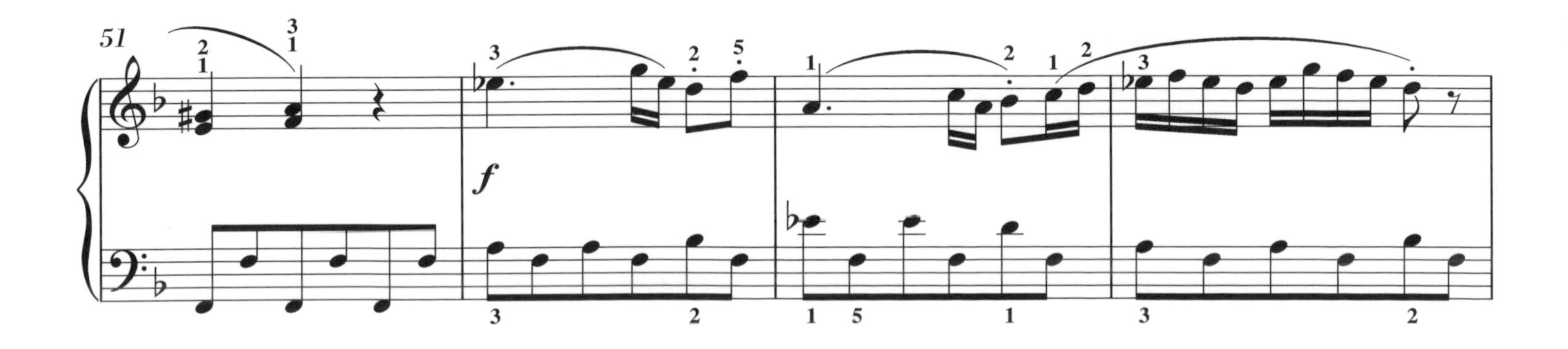
51
f

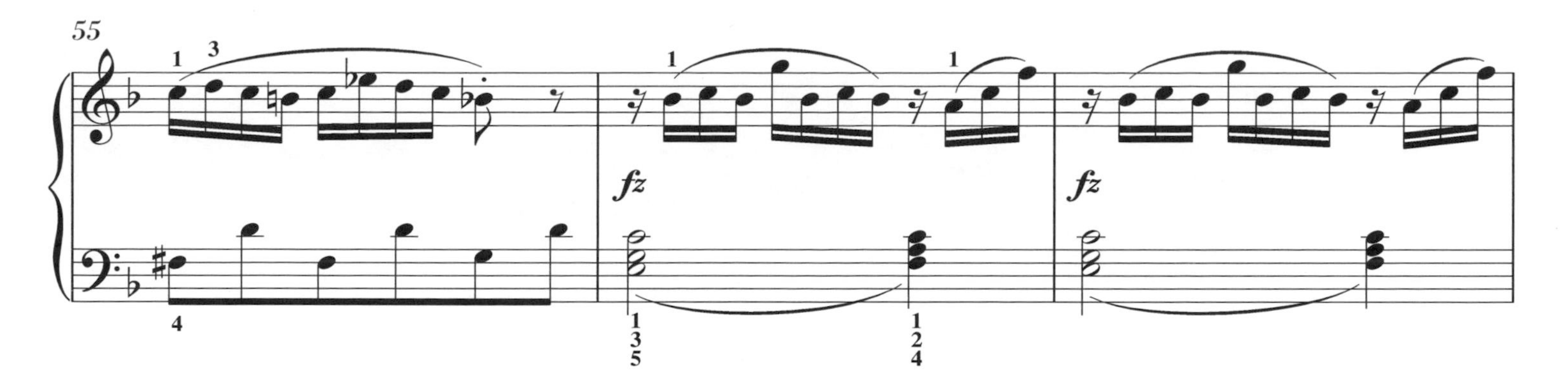
55
fz
fz

58
p
fz

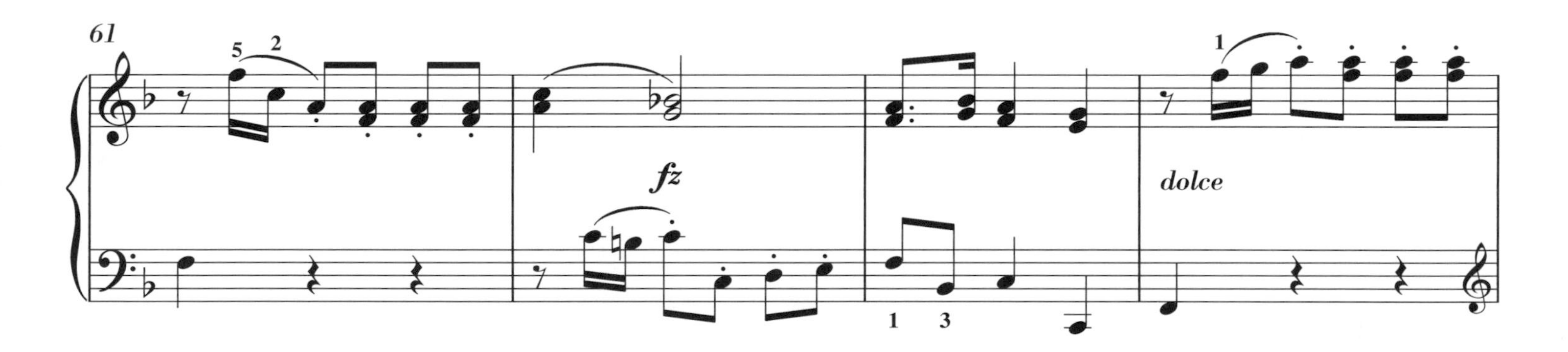
61
fz
dolce

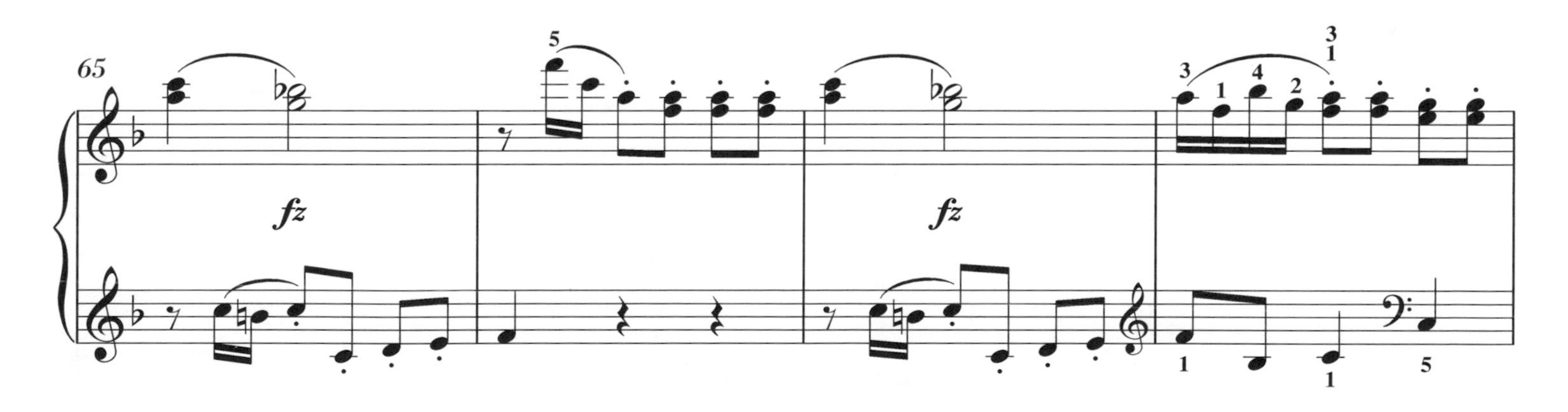
65
fz
fz

69

II

Andante con espressione [♩ = 46-58]

p

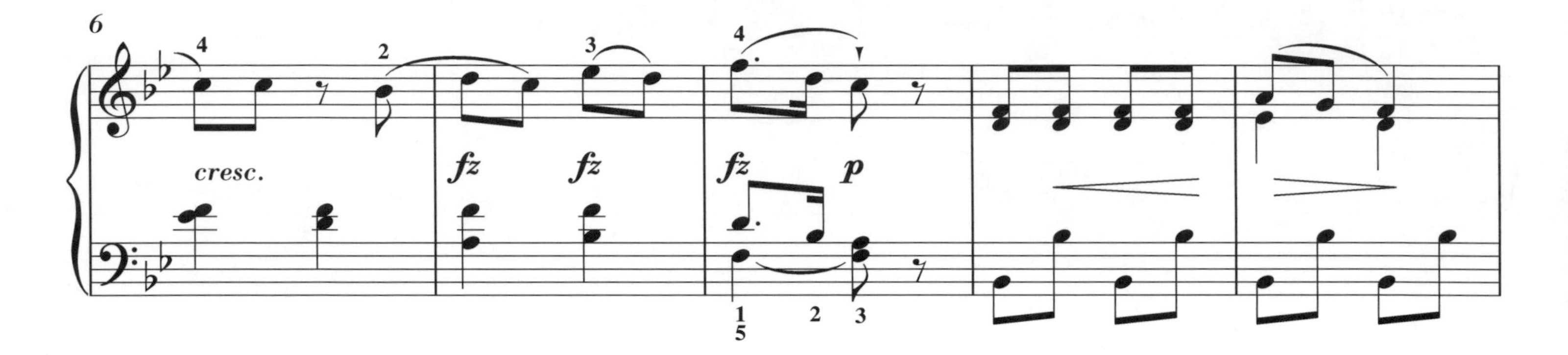

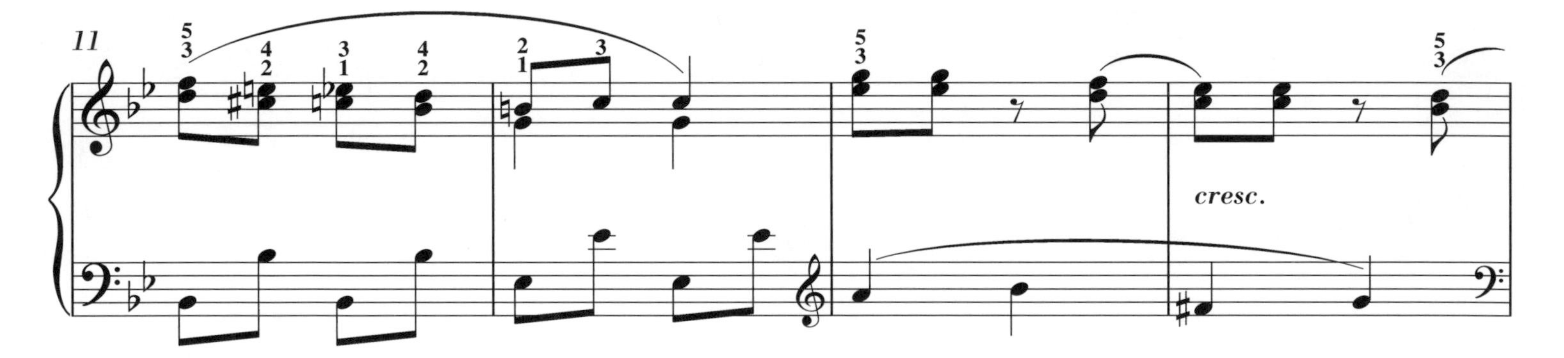

23
cresc.
f
dim.

27
p
fz
cresc.

33
fz
fz
fz
p
pp
cresc.

38
dolce
cresc.

42
f
cresc.
f
ff

III

Rondo

Allegro vivace [♩ = 72-88]

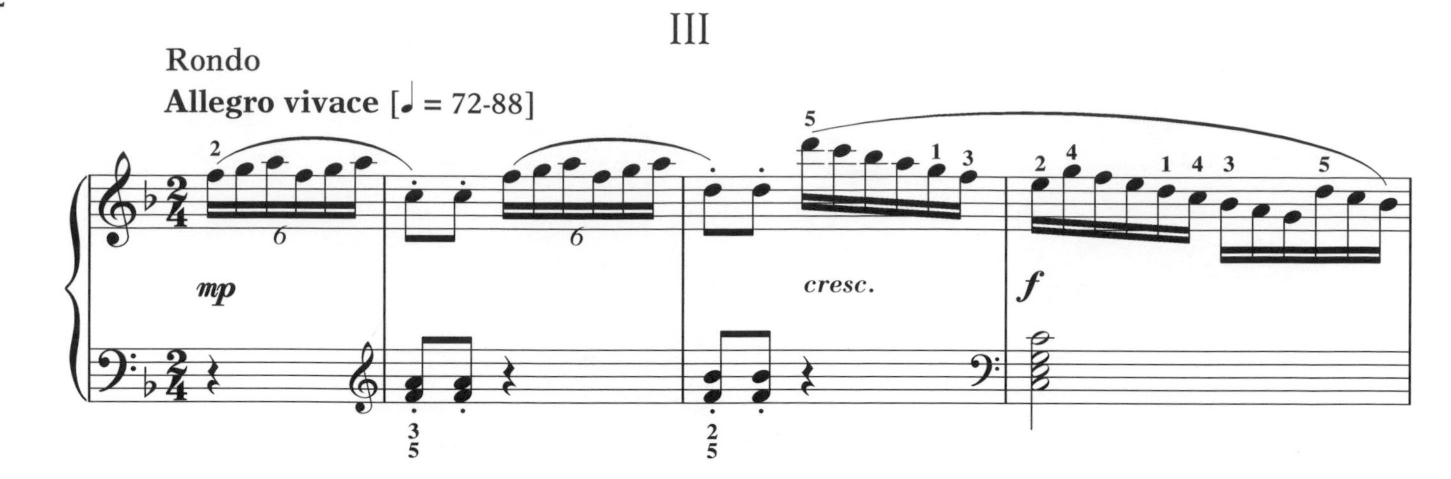

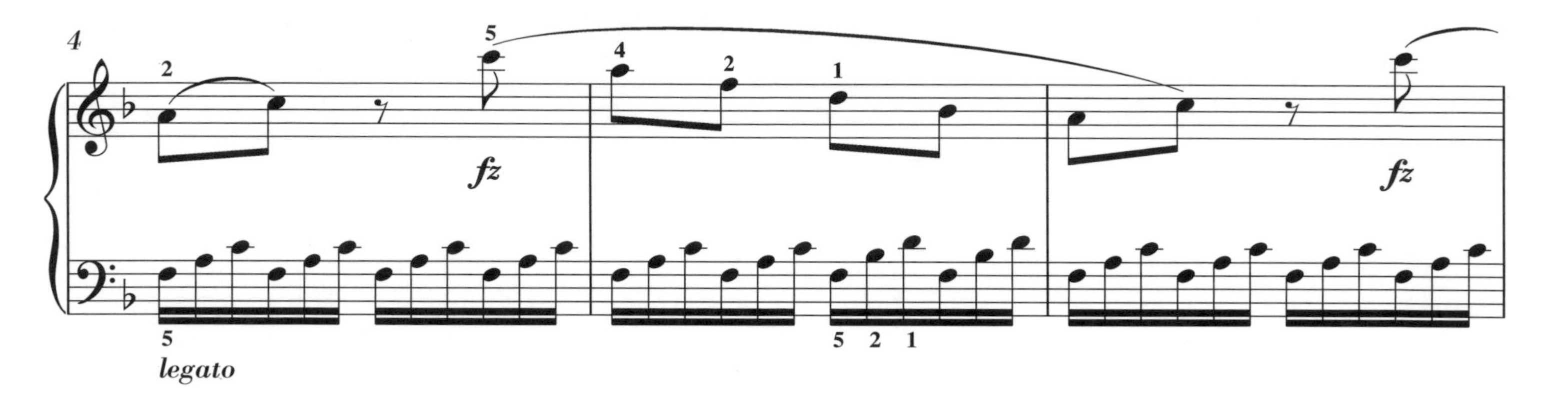

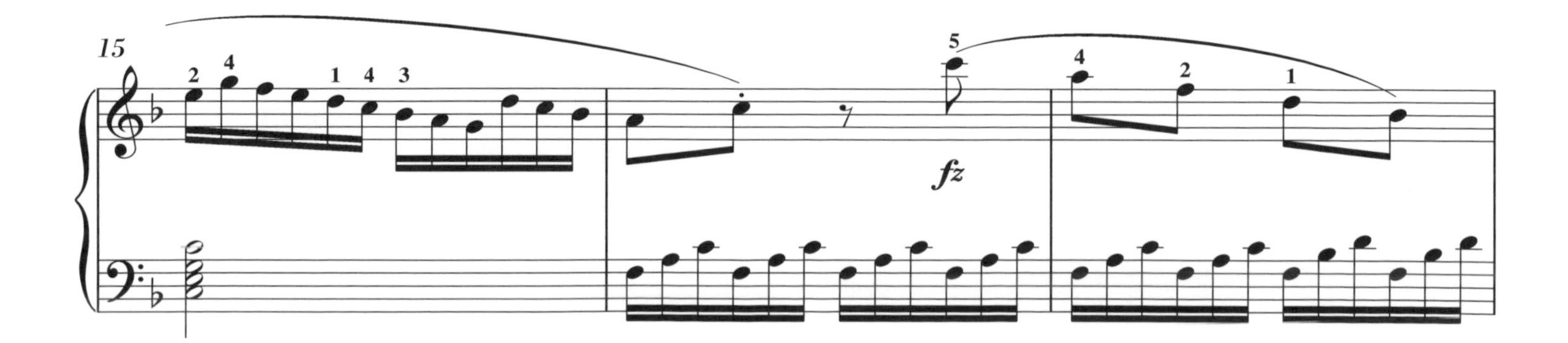

18
fz
fz

22
p
f

25
ff
Fine
p dolce

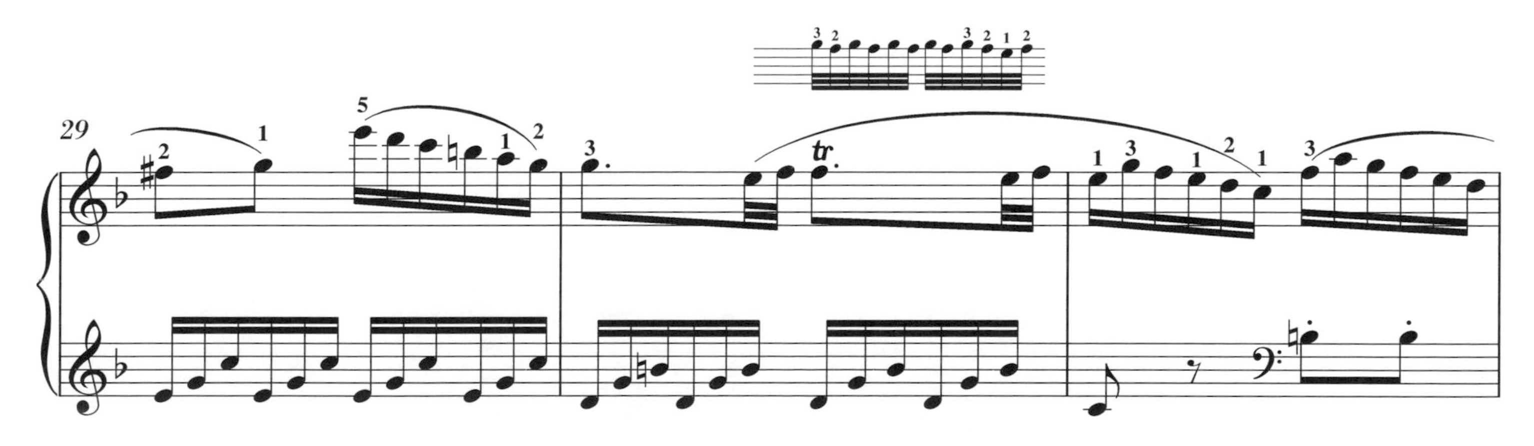
29
tr

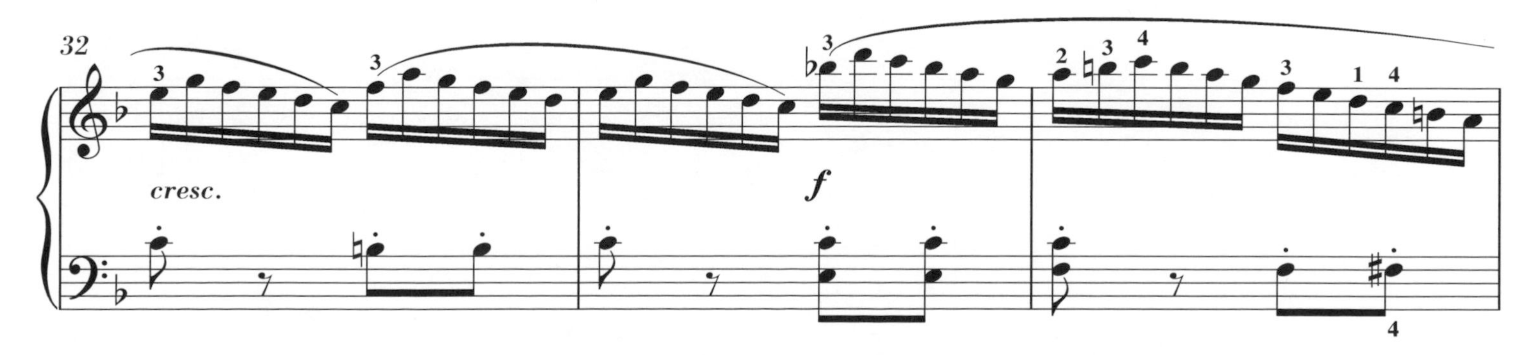
32
cresc.
f

35
tr
p

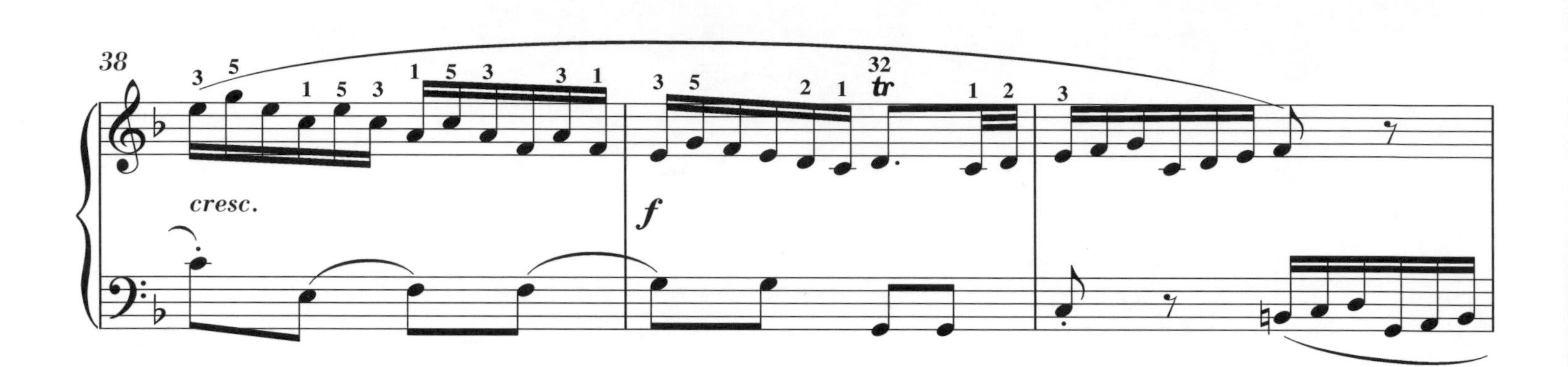
38
tr
cresc.
f

41
f

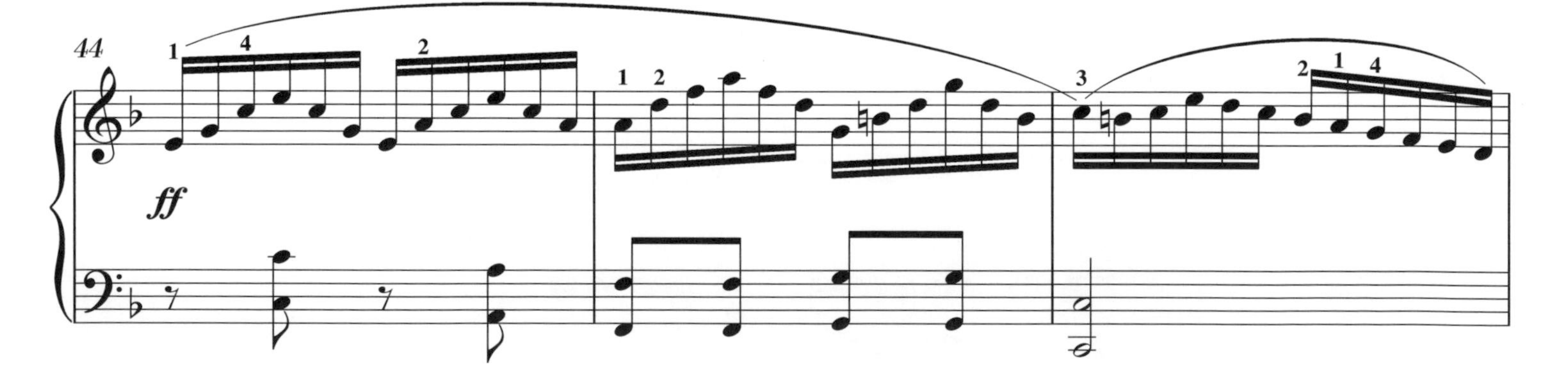
44
ff

47
D.C. al Fine
dim.

LABORUM
DULCE
LENIMEN
G. SCHIRMER

Sonatina in G Major

I

Muzio Clementi
Op. 36, No. 5

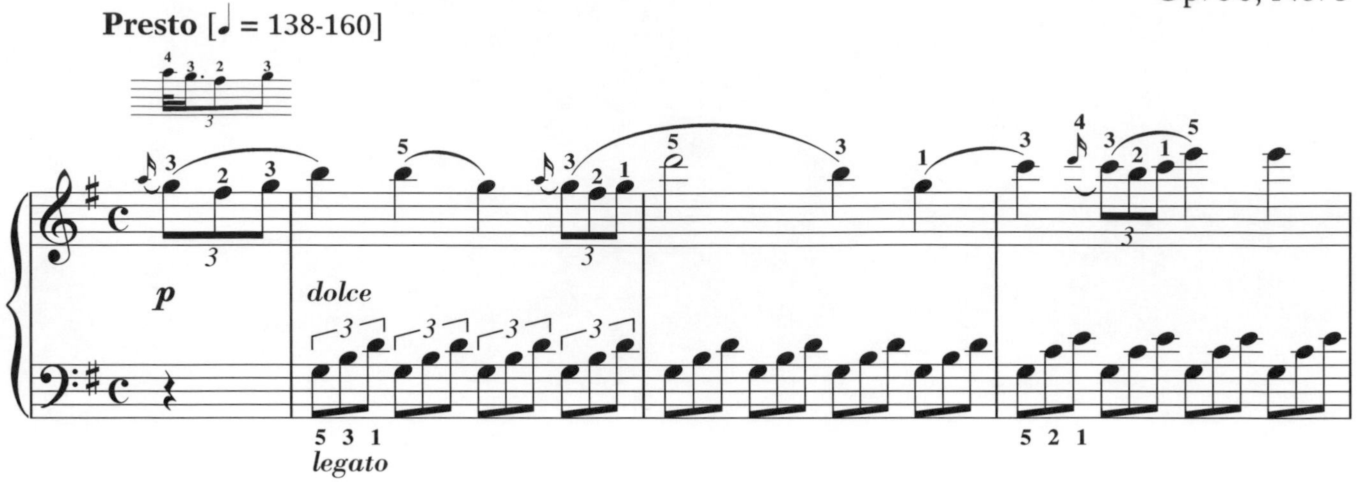

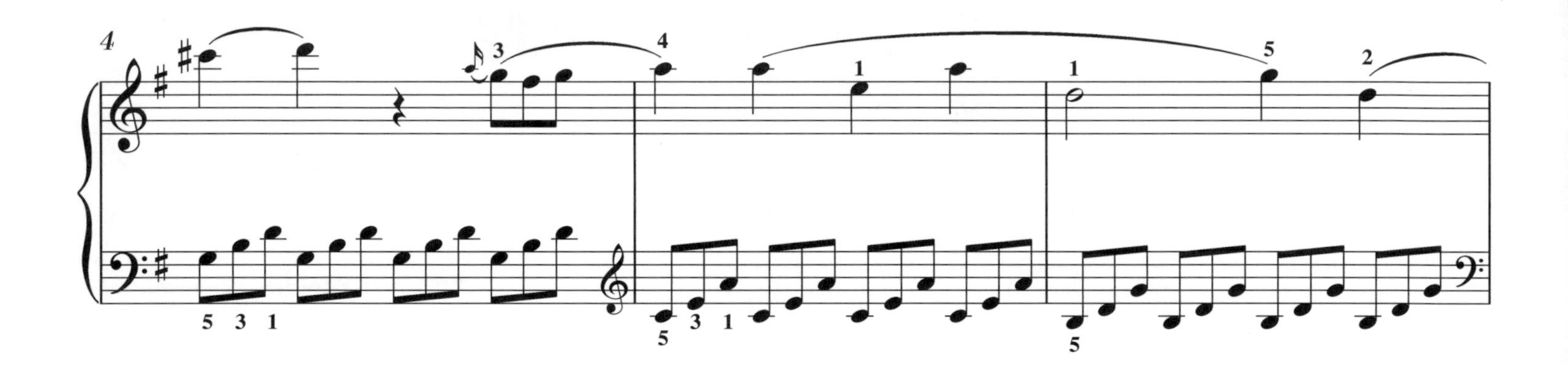

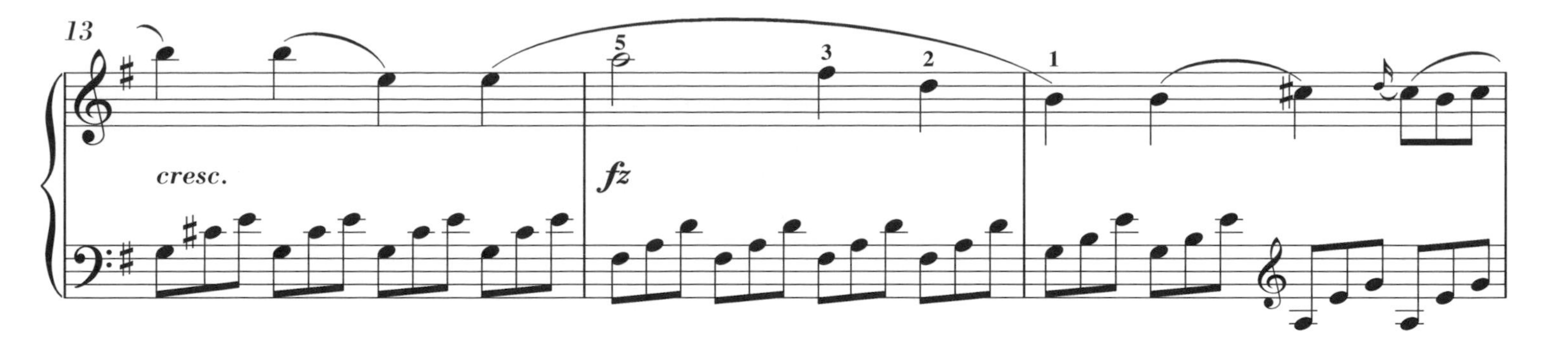
13
cresc.
fz

16

19

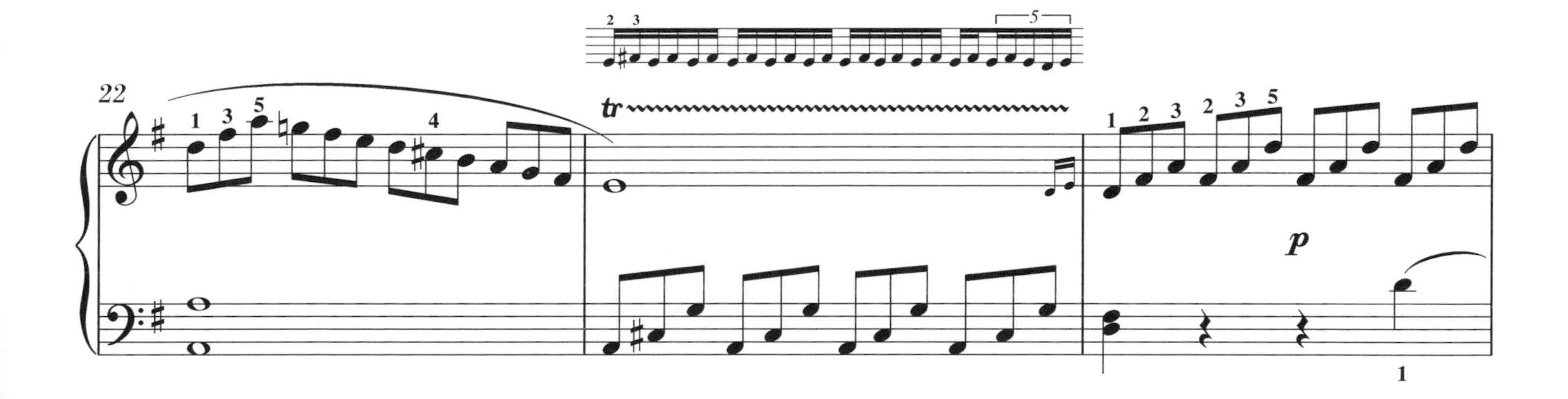
22
tr
p

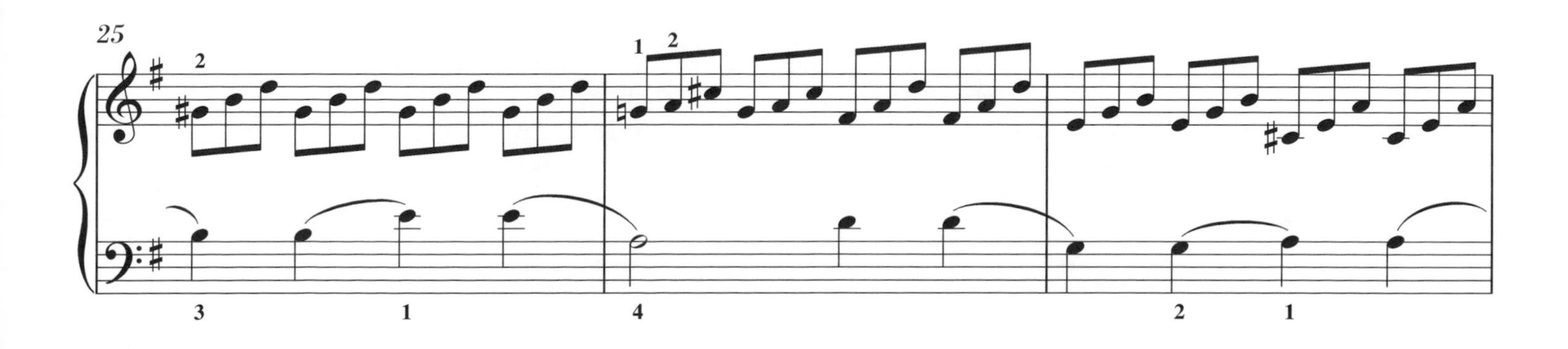
25

28
cresc.
fz
cresc.

32
fz

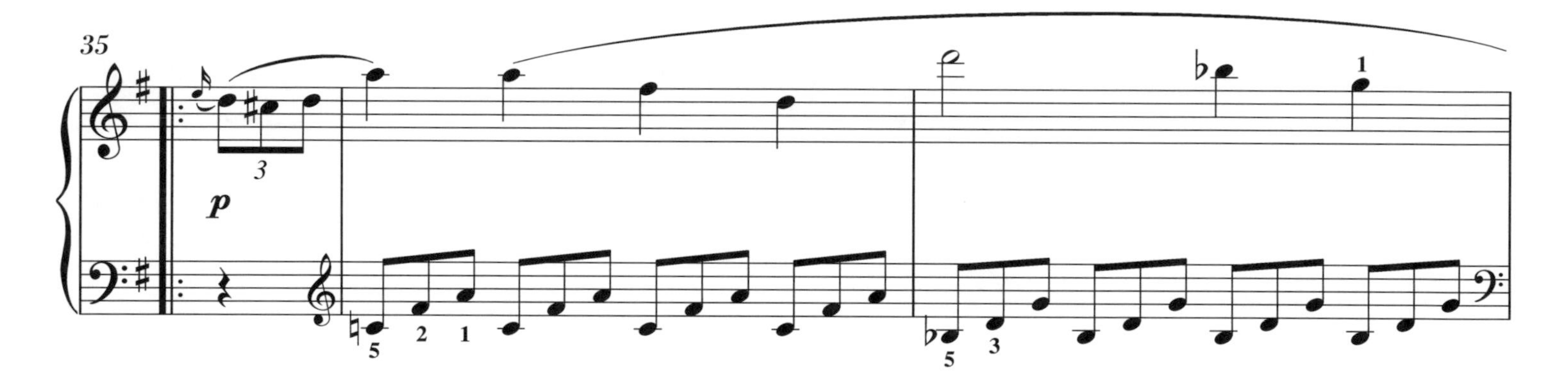
35
p

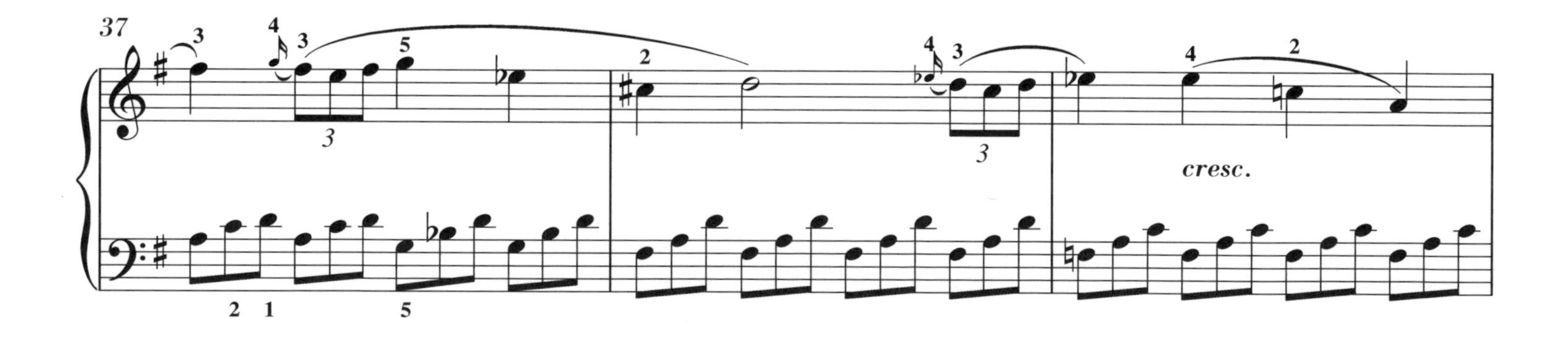
37
cresc.

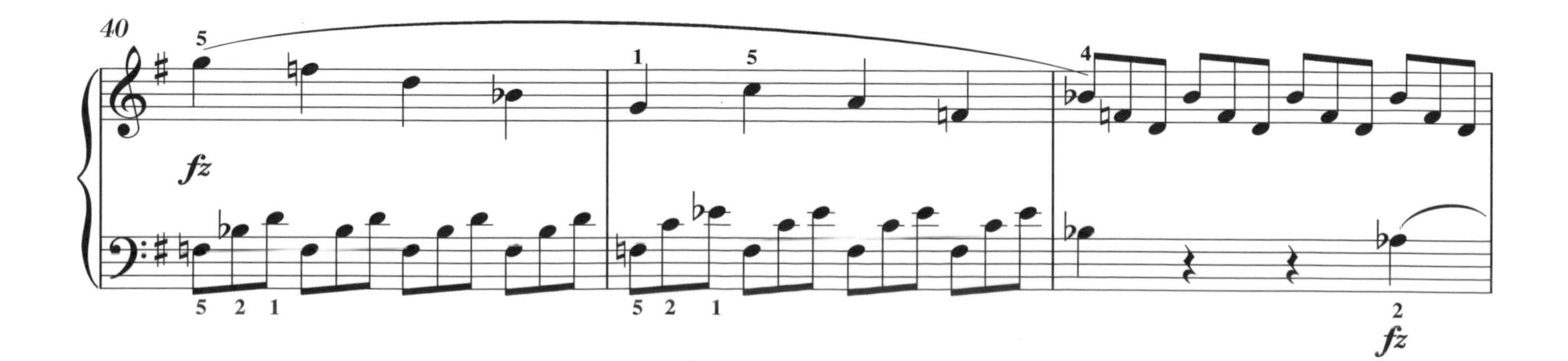
40
fz
fz

43
fz

46
ff

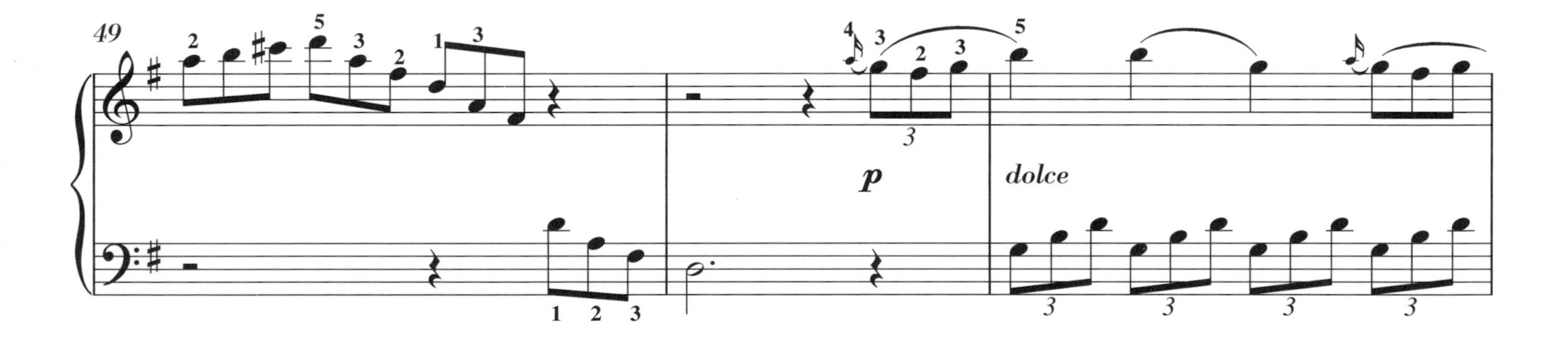
49
p
dolce

52

55

58
fz
fz

61
fz
f

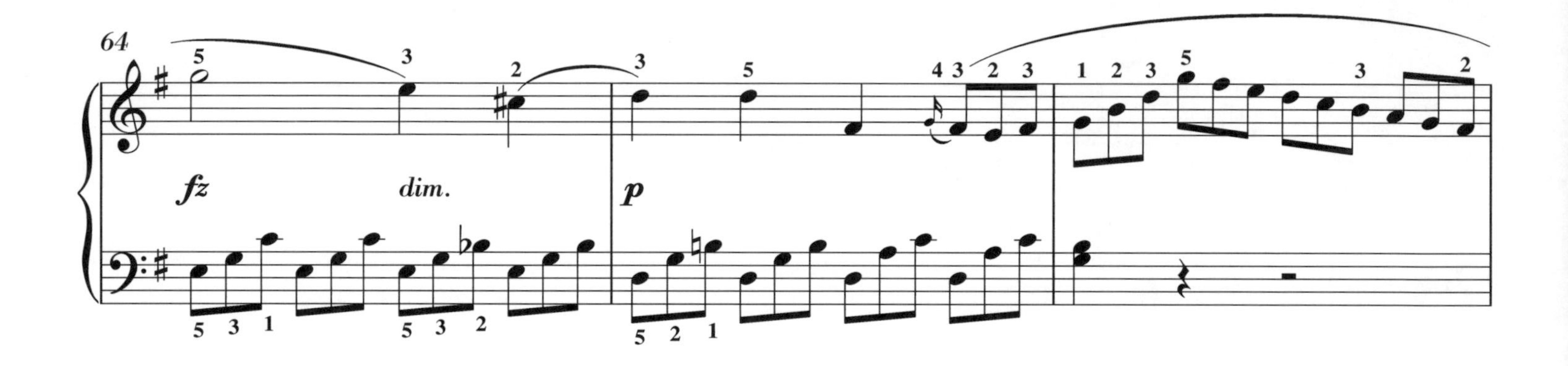
64
fz
dim.
p

67

70
f

73
tr
p

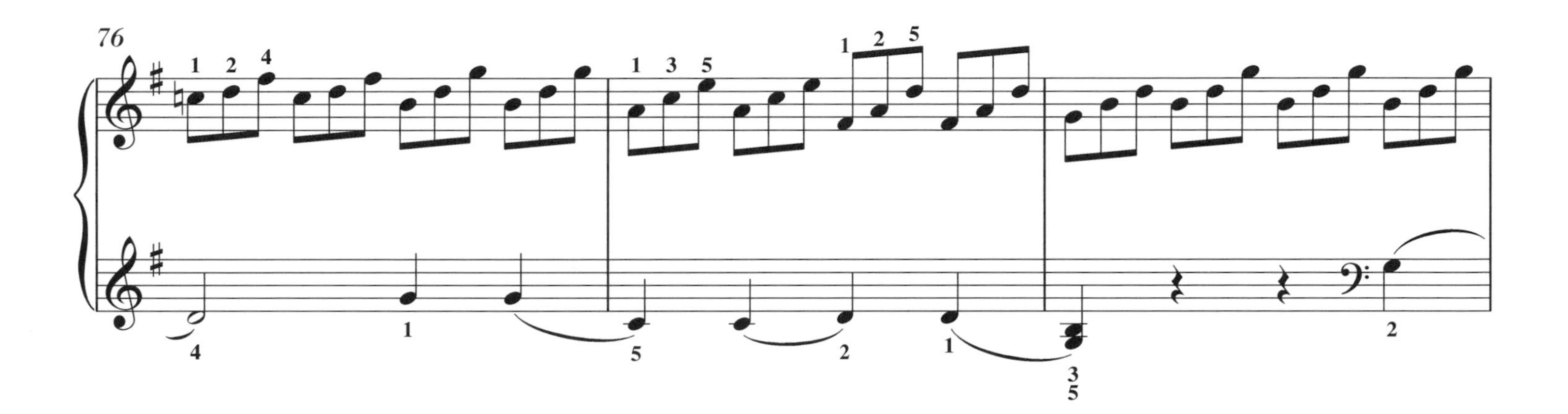
76

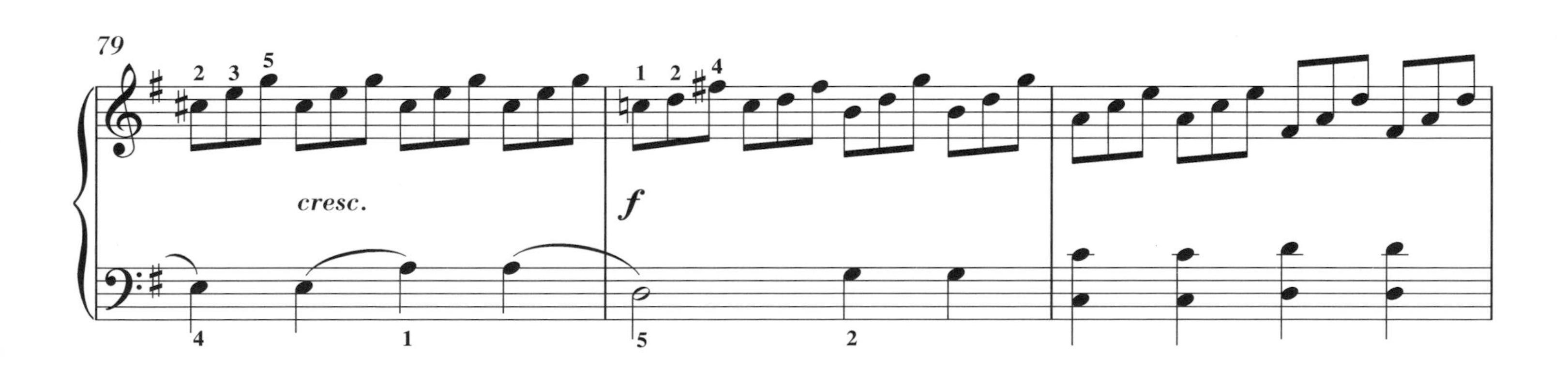
79
cresc.
f

82
fz
fz

II

Air suisse original

Allegretto moderato [♩. = 52-63]

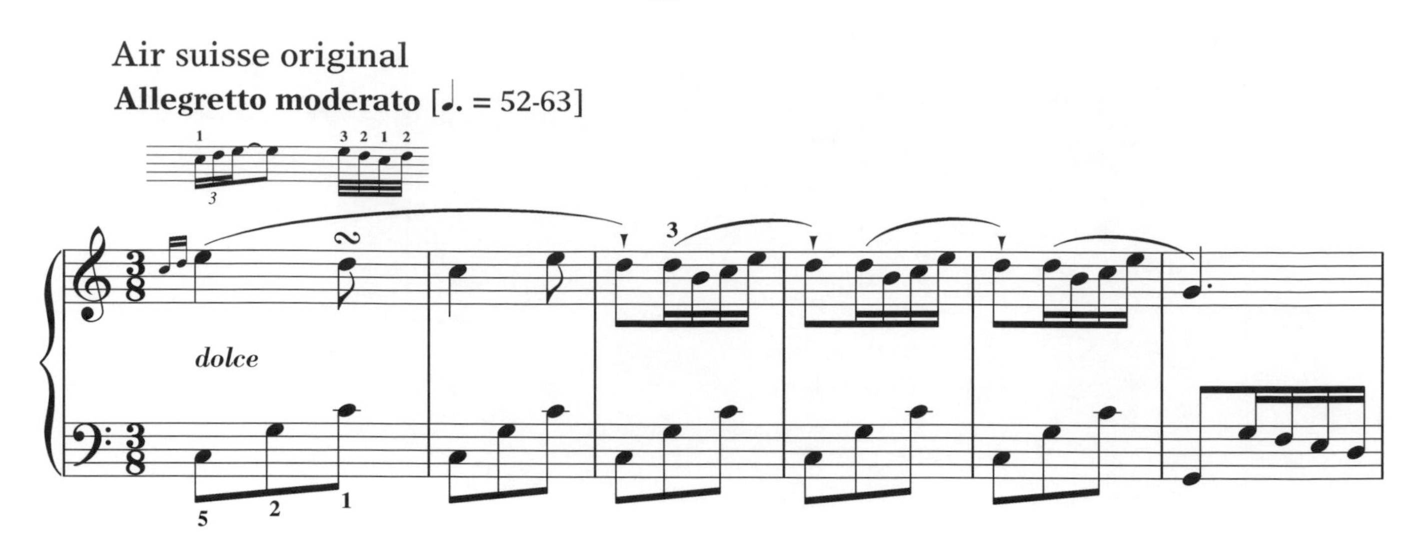

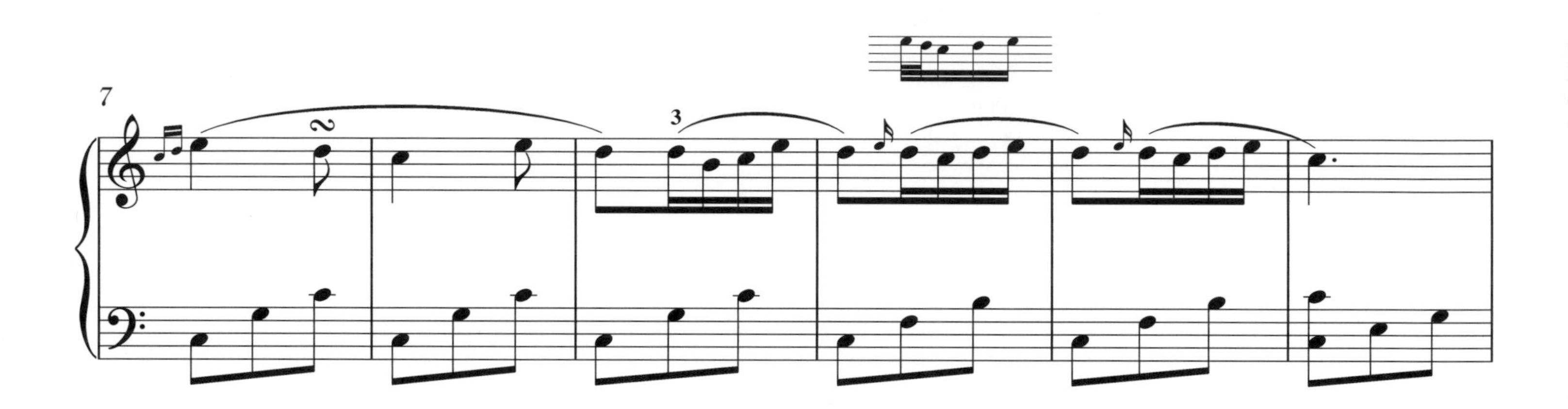

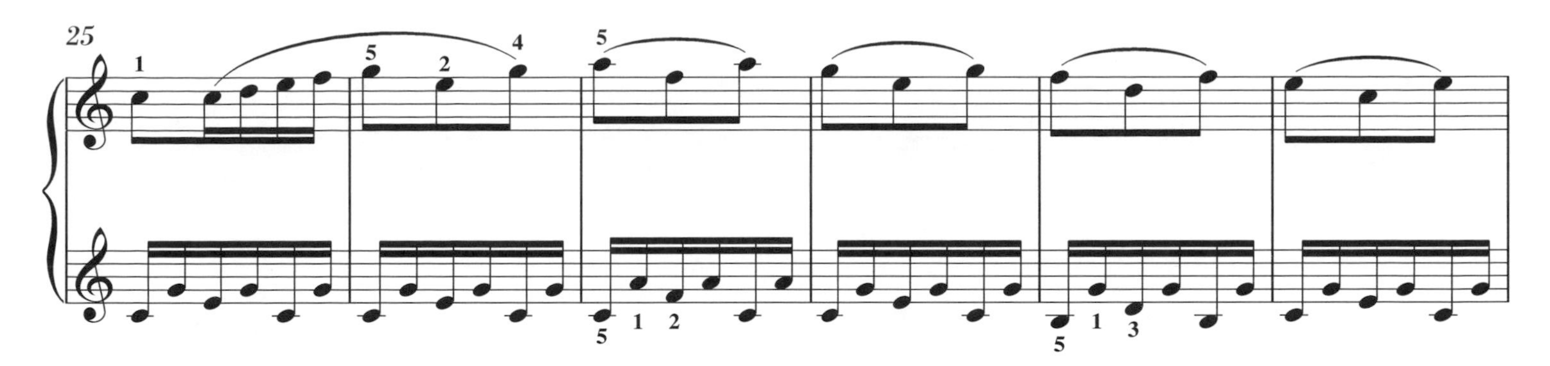
25

31

37
p

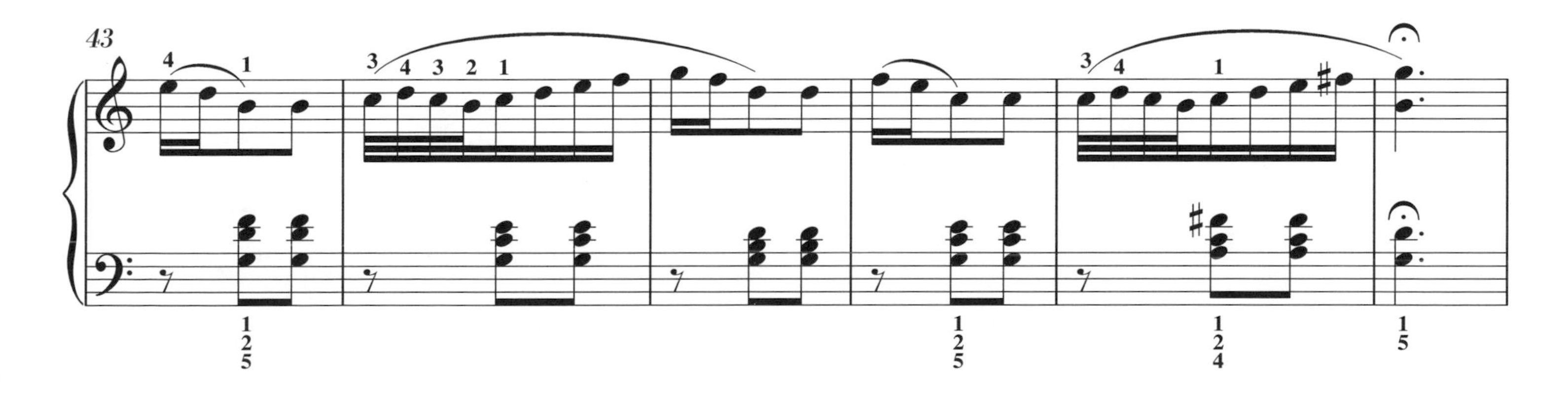
43

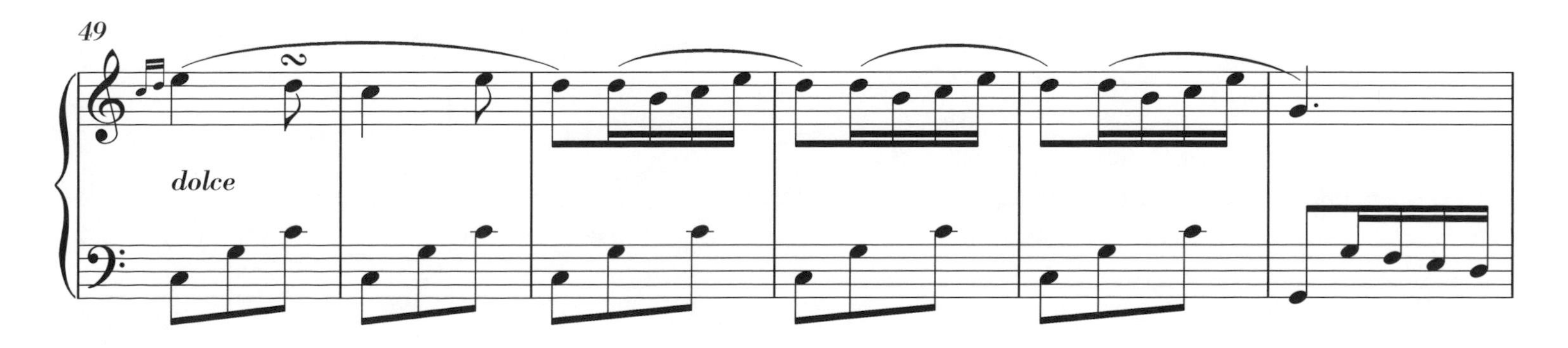
49
dolce

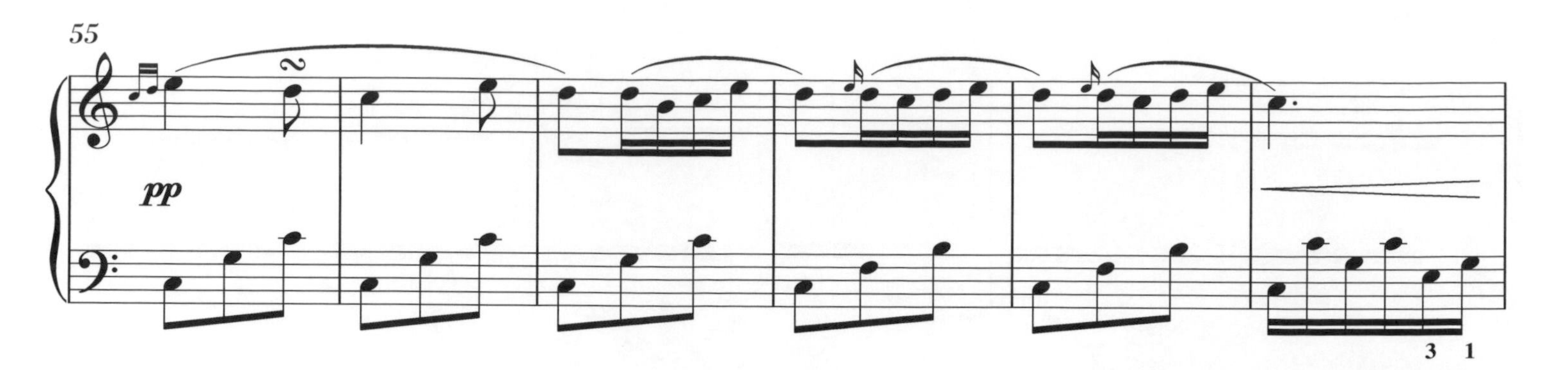
55
pp

61
f

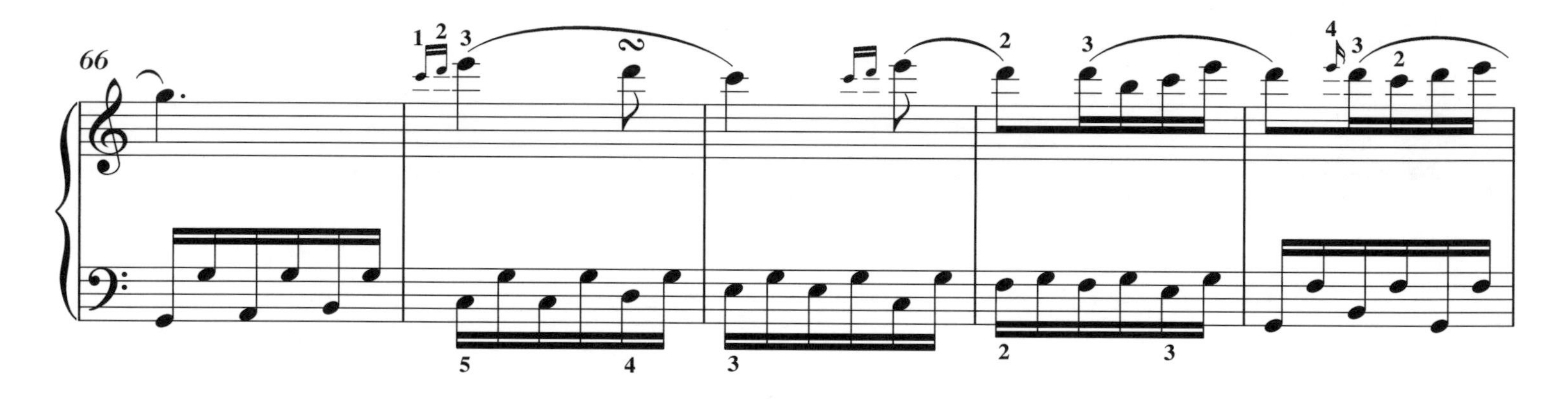
66

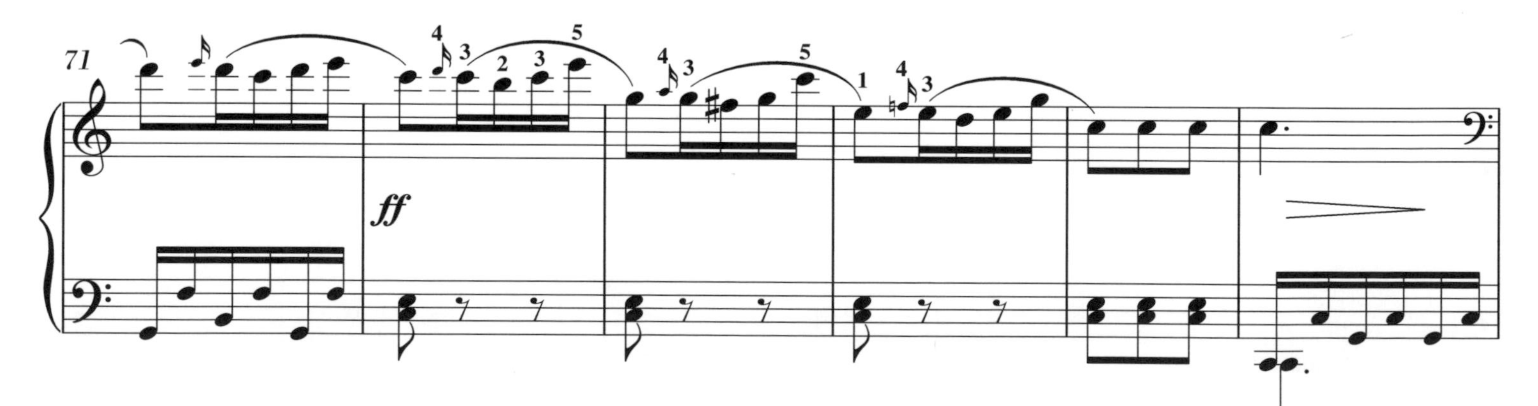
71
ff

77
p
pp

III

Rondo

Allegro di molto [♩ = 104-126]

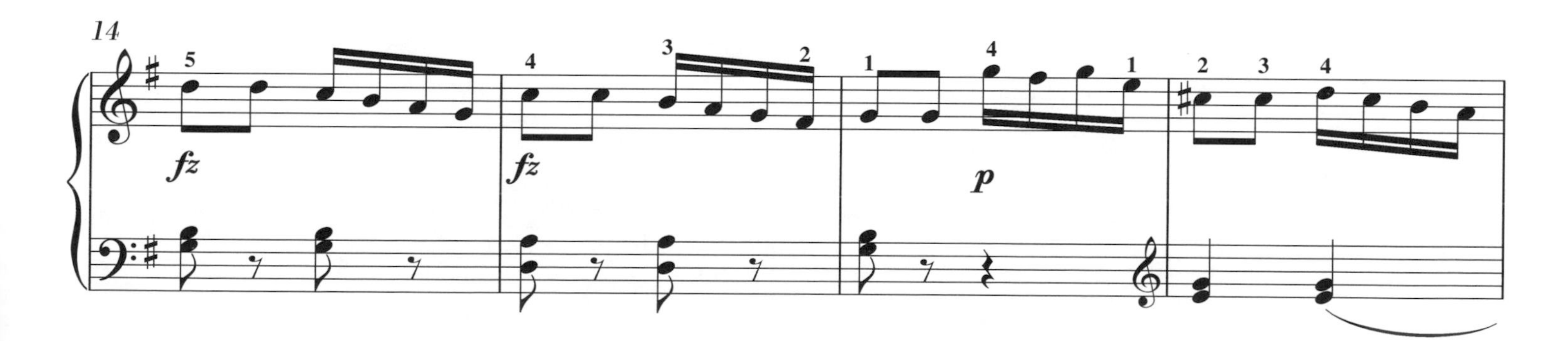

dim.
p

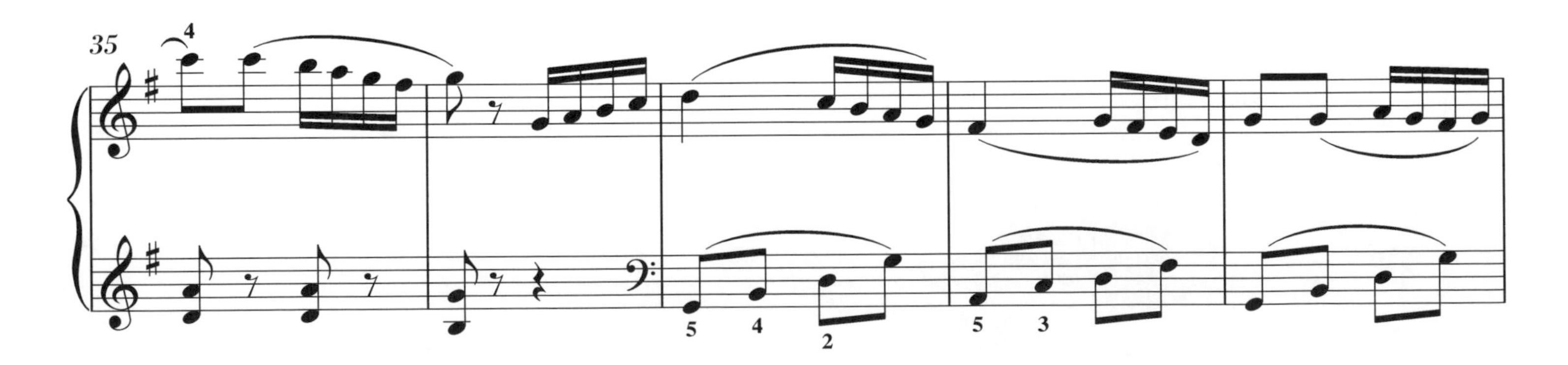

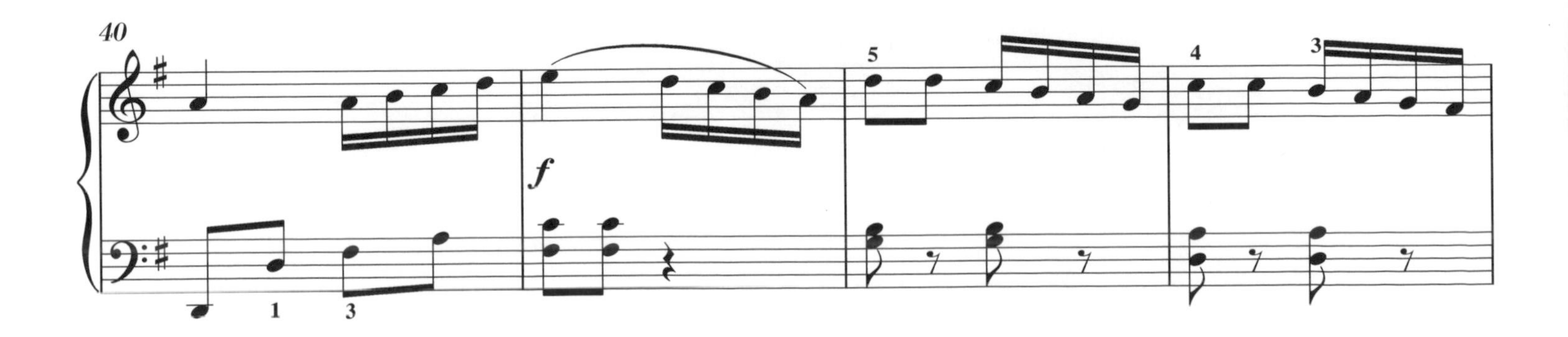
f

44
dim.
p
cresc.

49
f
p
p

54
Fine
f

59
p

63

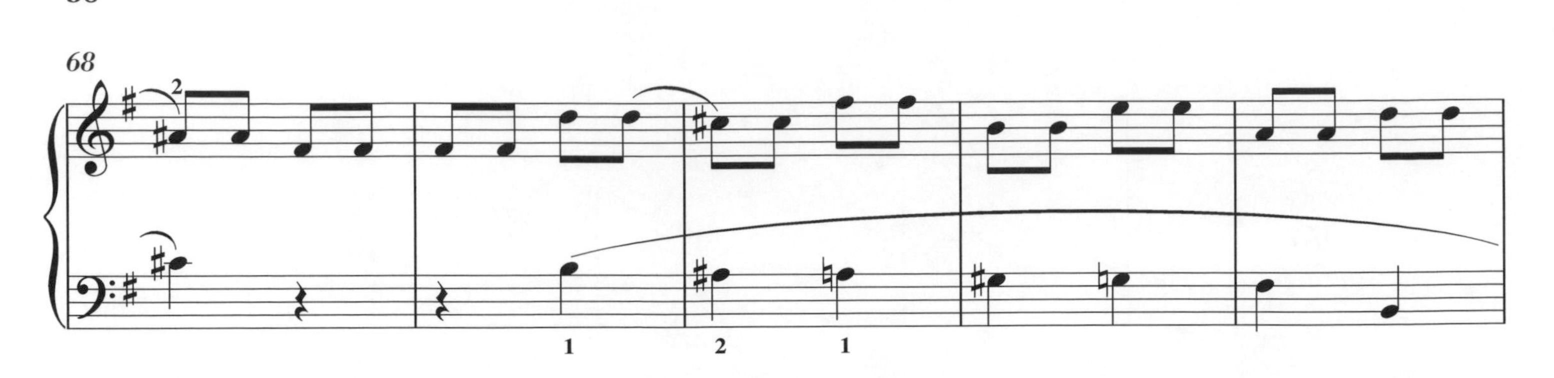

f
fz
fz
fz

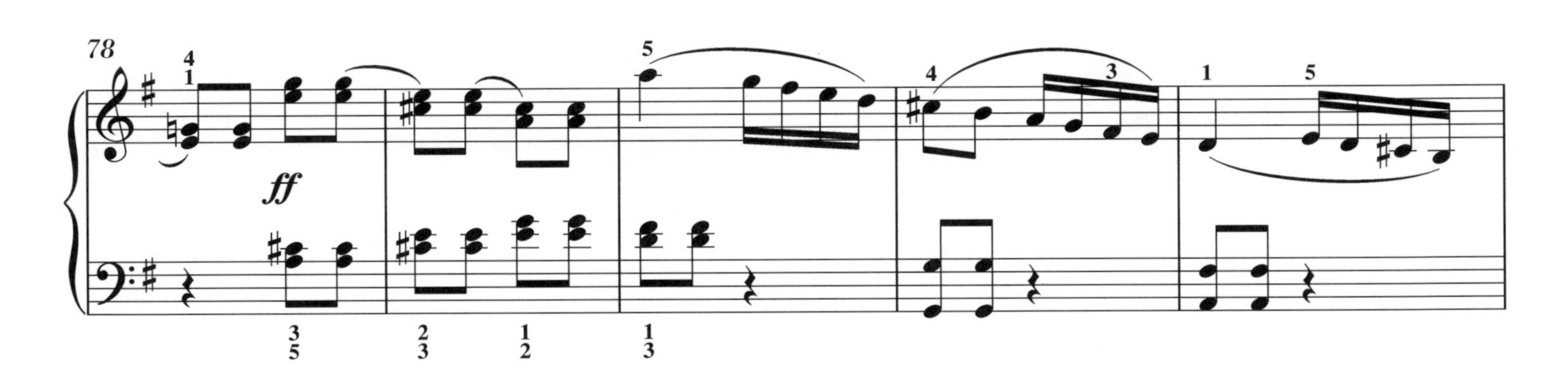
ff

p
pp

cresc.
fz
fz
fz
fz

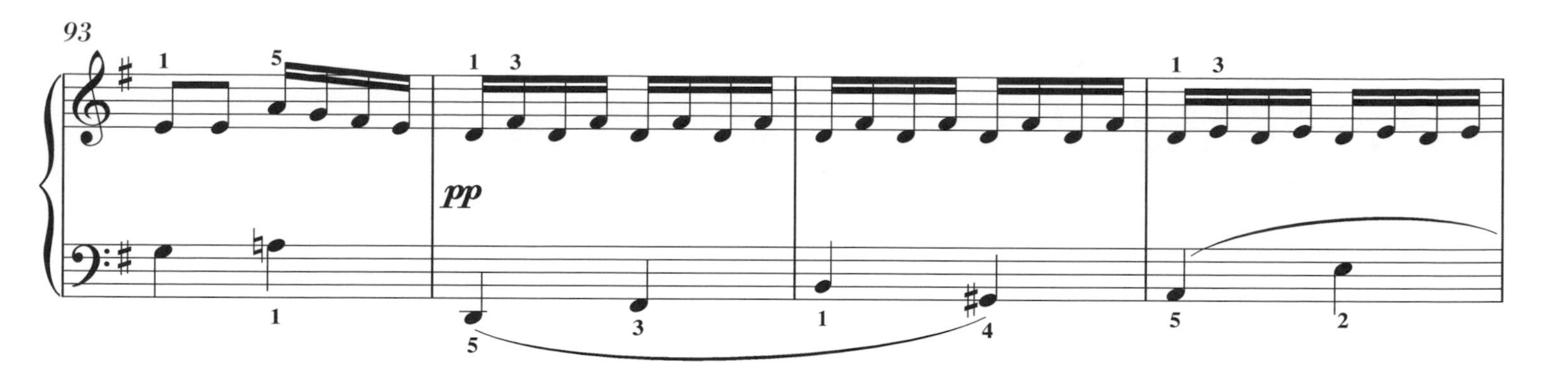
93
pp

97
cresc.
f

101

105
p
pp

109
D.C. al Fine

LABORUM
DULCE
LENIMEN
G. SCHIRMER

Sonatina in D Major

I

Muzio Clementi
Op. 36, No. 6

Allegro con spirito [♩ = 112-126]

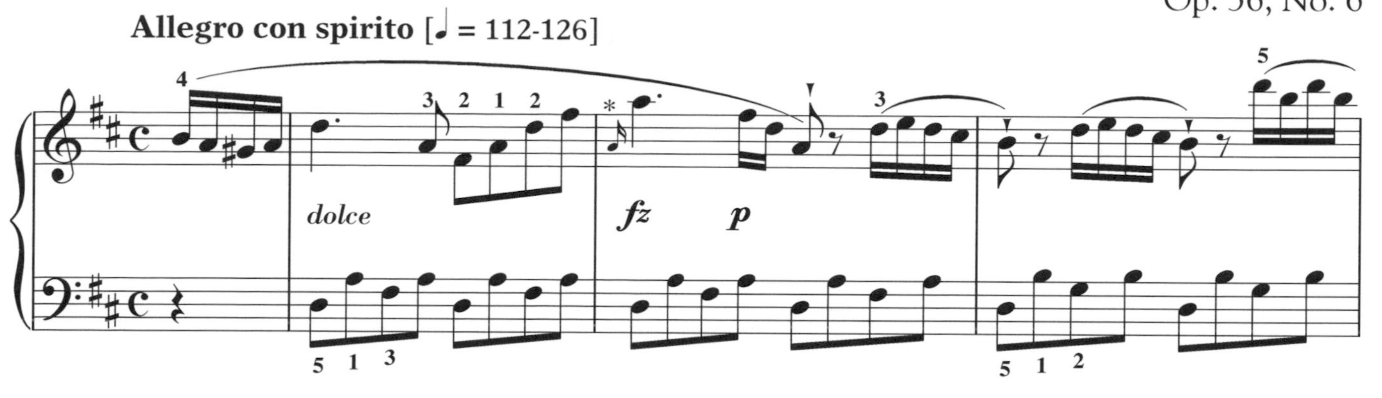

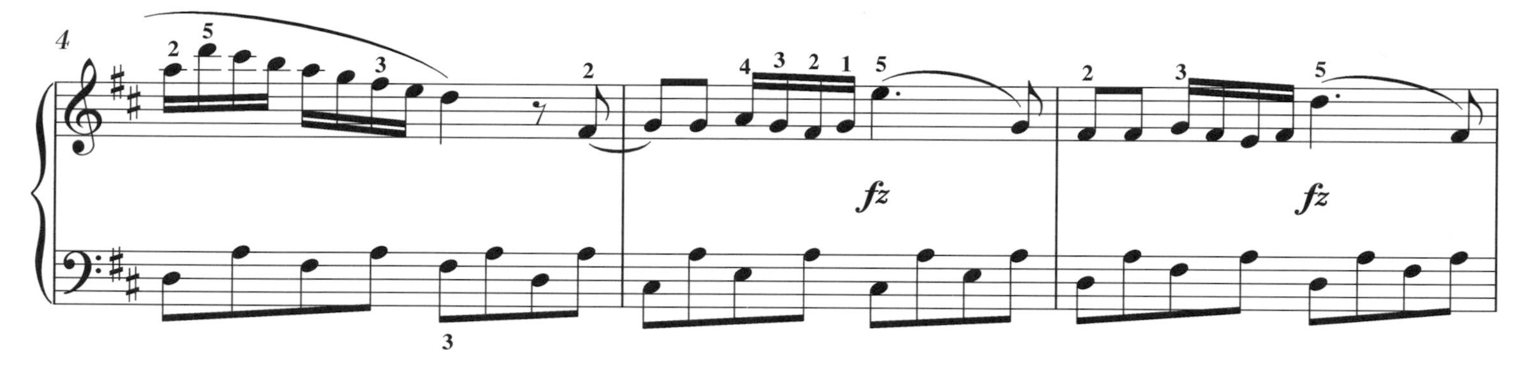

*play the appoggiatura quickly, on the beat

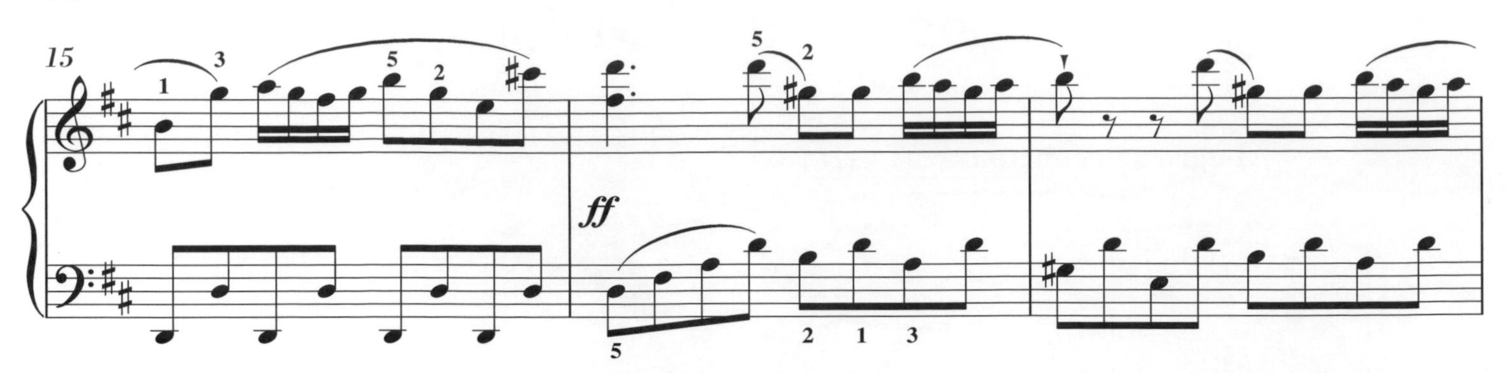
15
ff

18

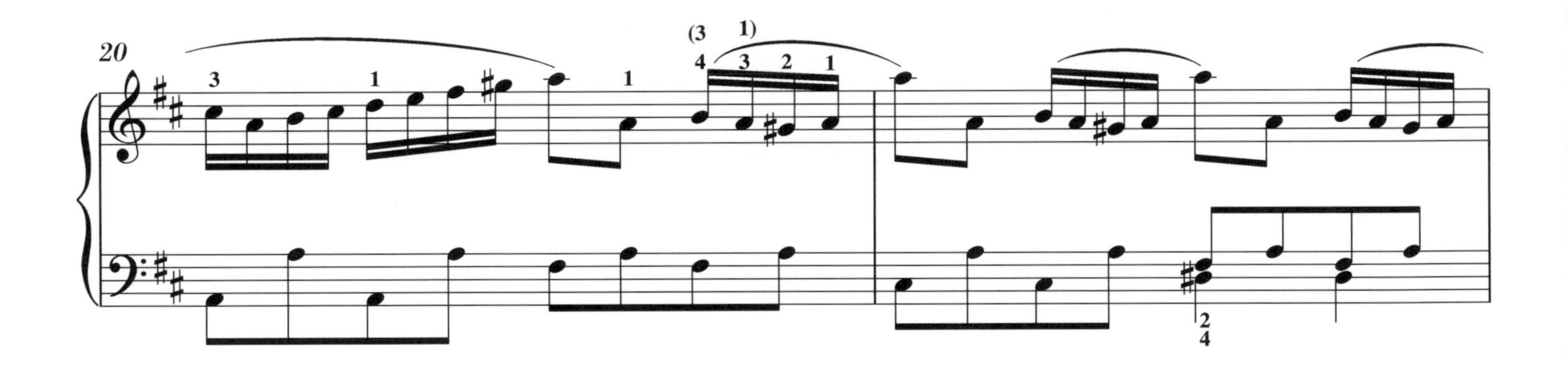
20

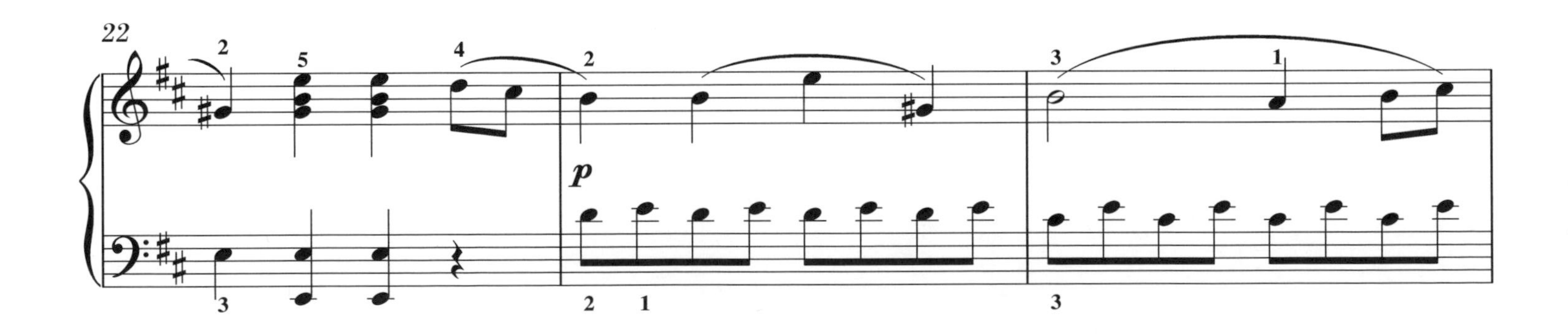
22
p

25
fz

ff

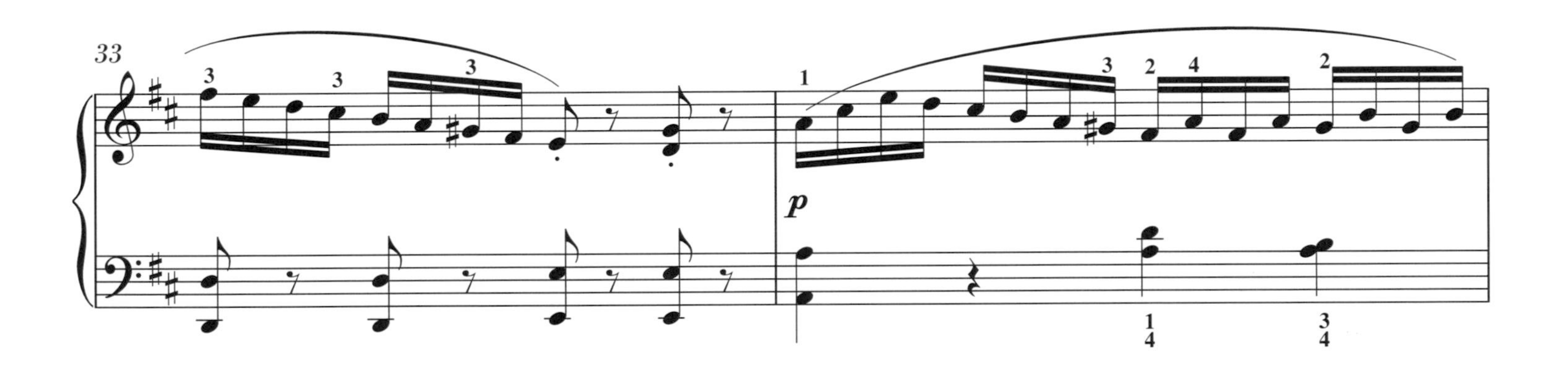
p

cresc.
f

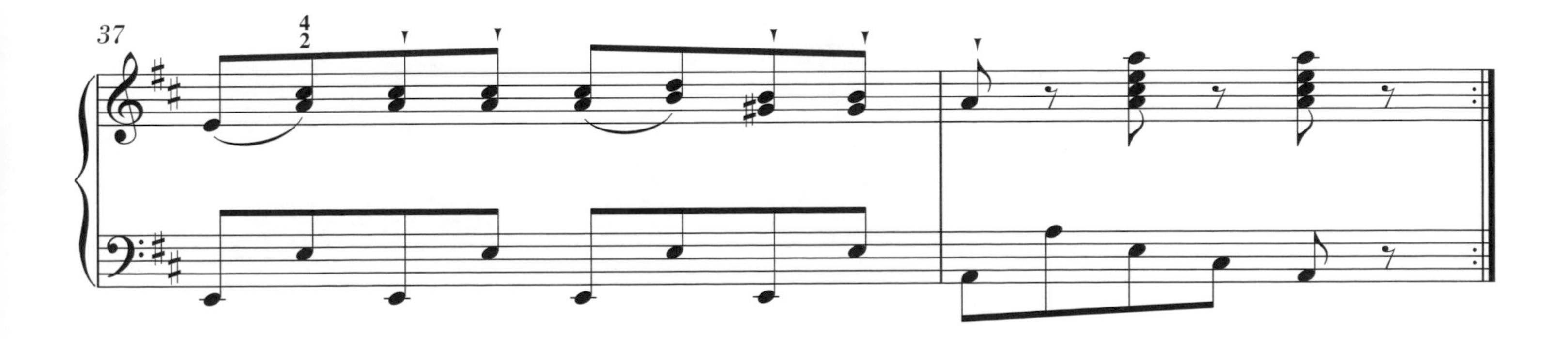

39
p

42
f
p

45
cresc.

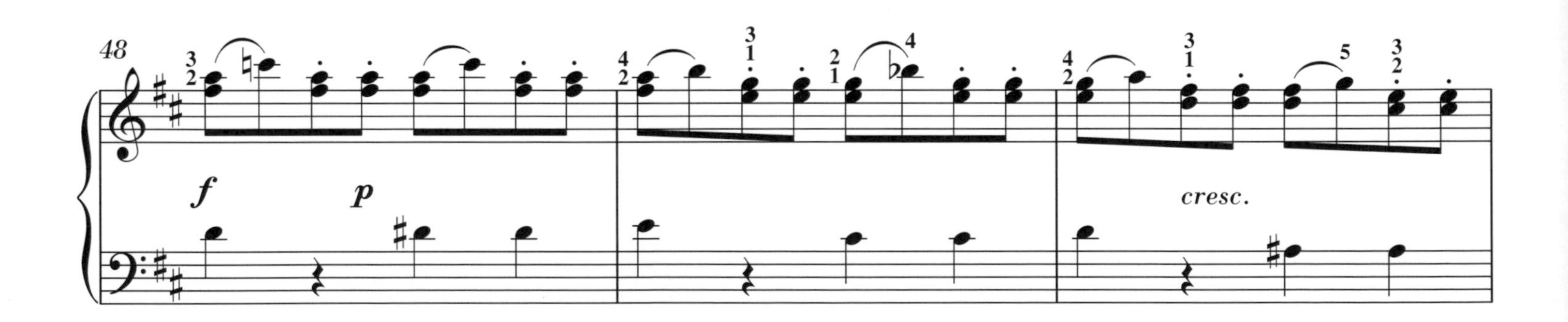
48
f
p
cresc.

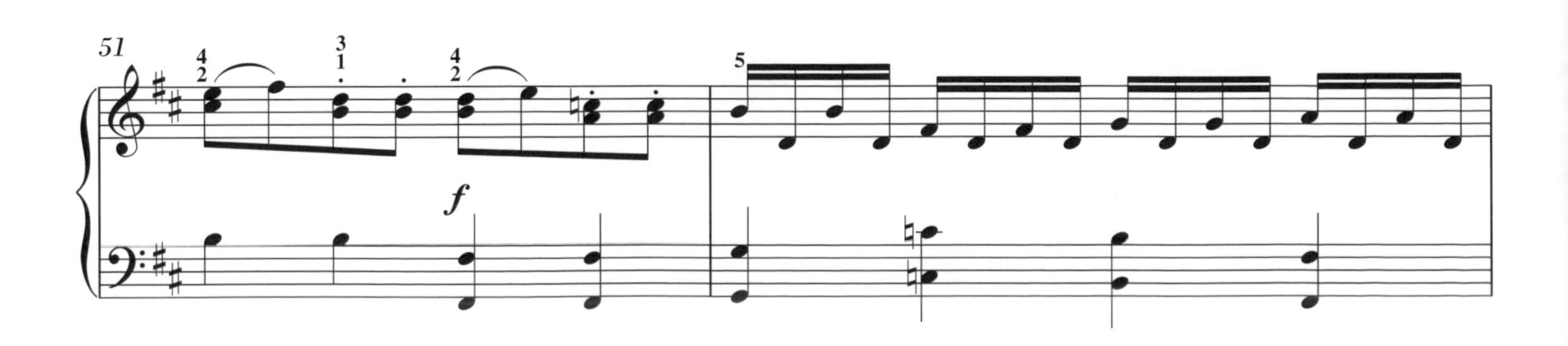
51
f

53
ff

55
dim.
p
dolce

58
fz
p
p

61
f

64
cresc.

66
f

68
ff
fz

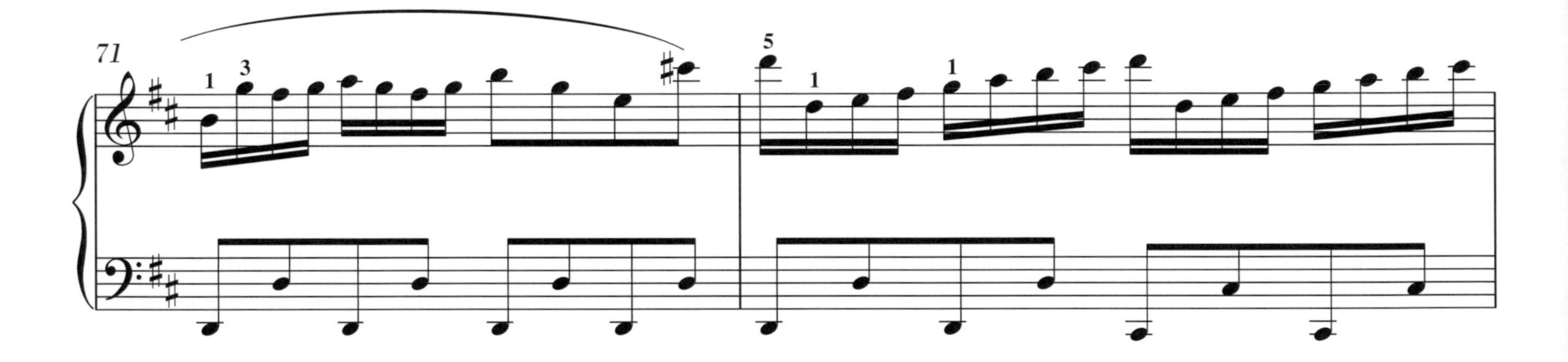
71

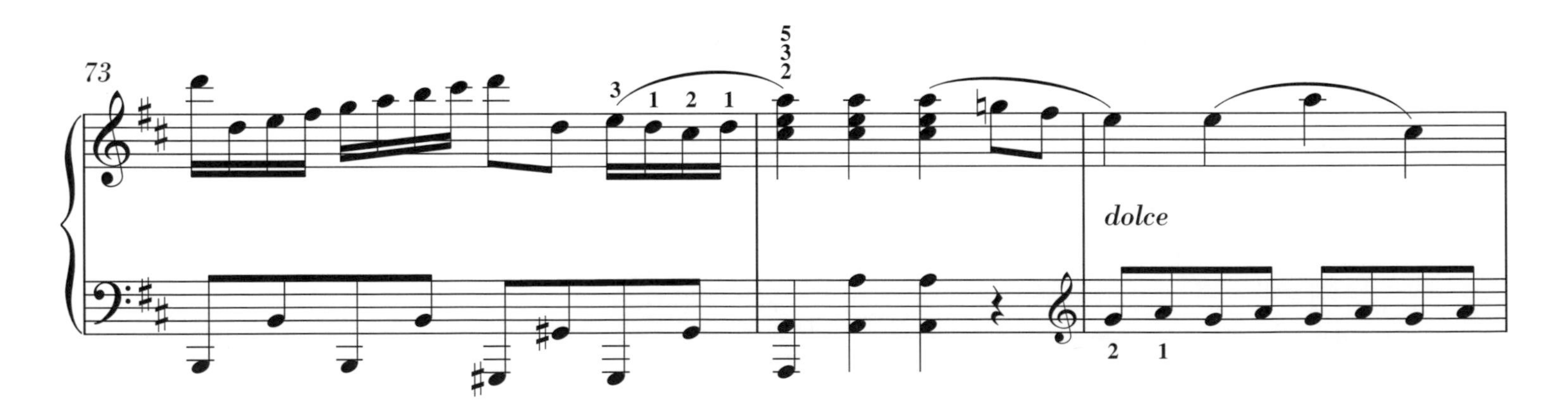
73
dolce

76

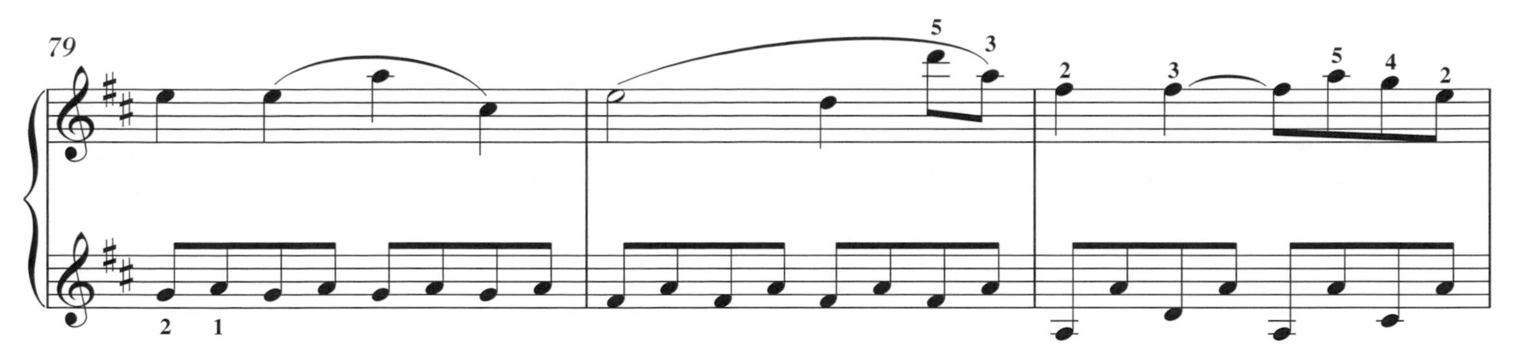
79

82
f

84
ff

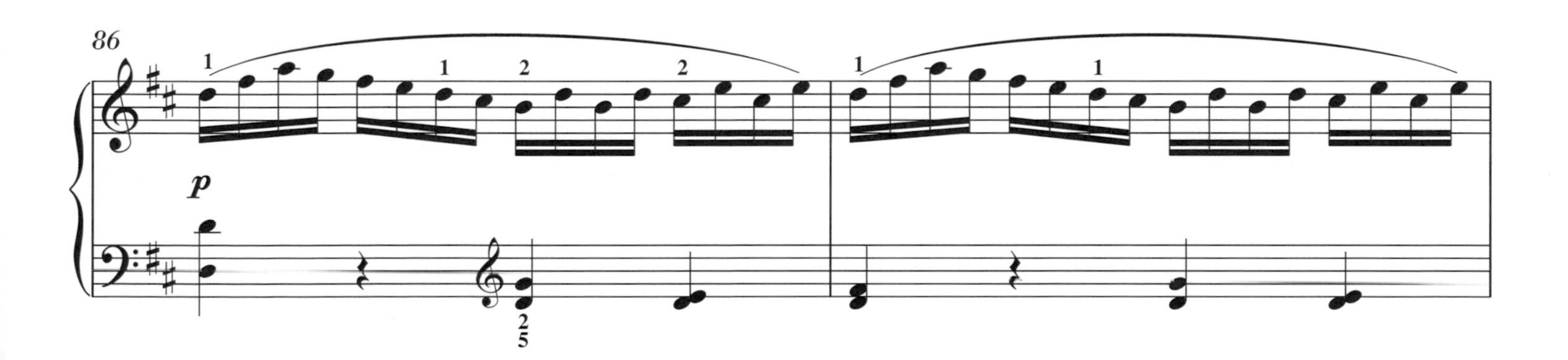
86
p

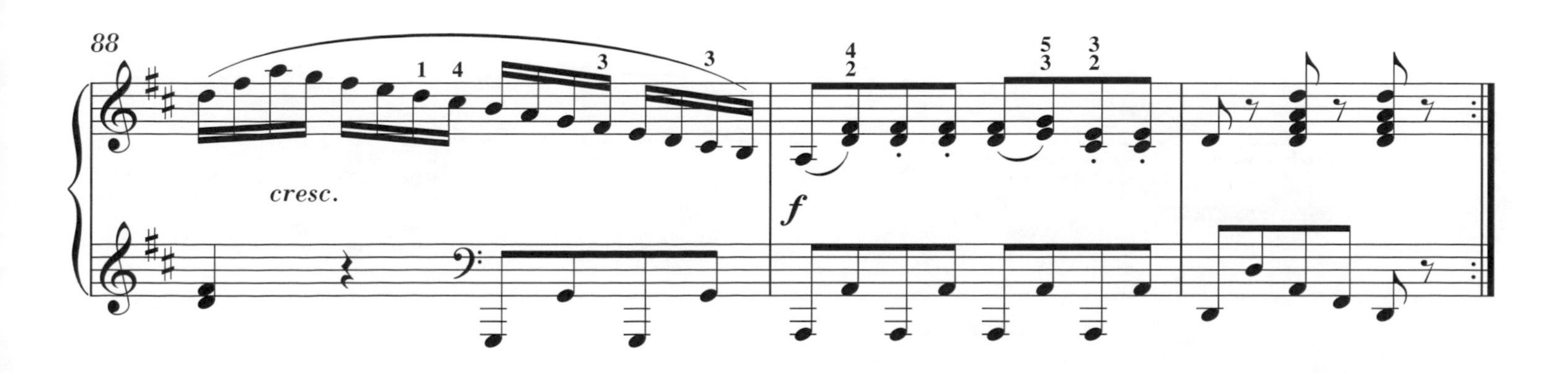
88
cresc.
f

II

Rondo

Allegro spiritoso [♩. = 69-84]

18
f

21
ff
Fine

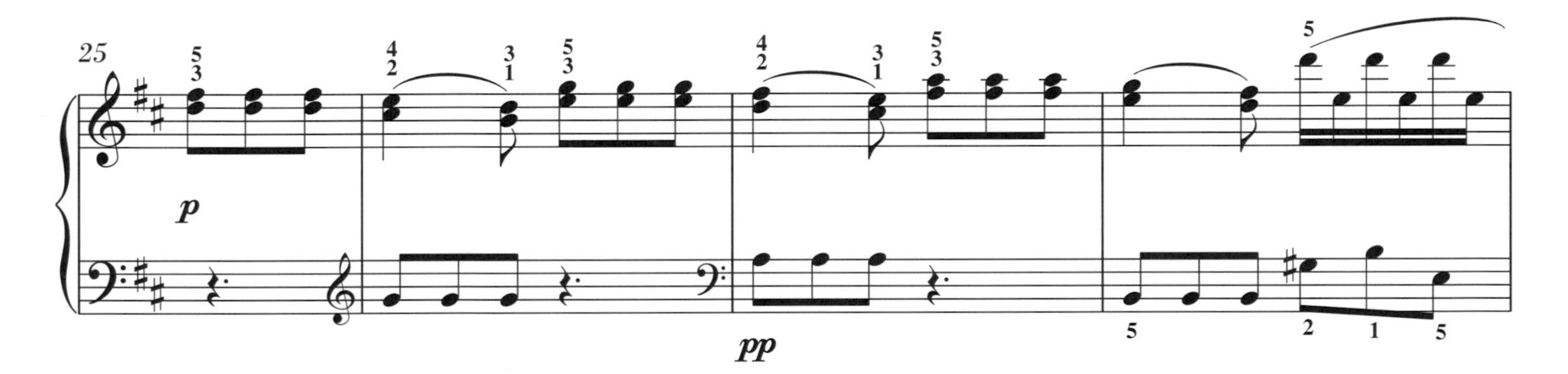
25
p
pp

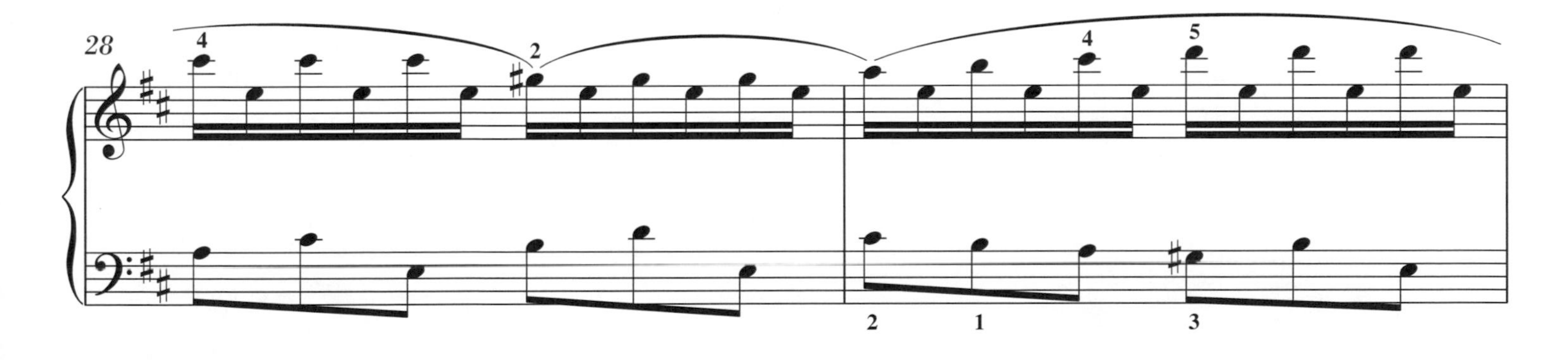
28

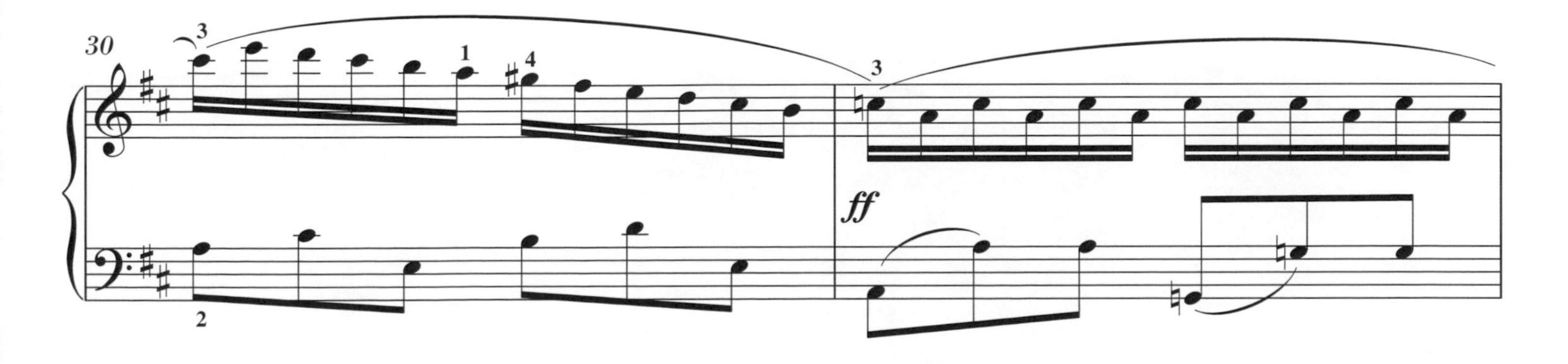
30
ff

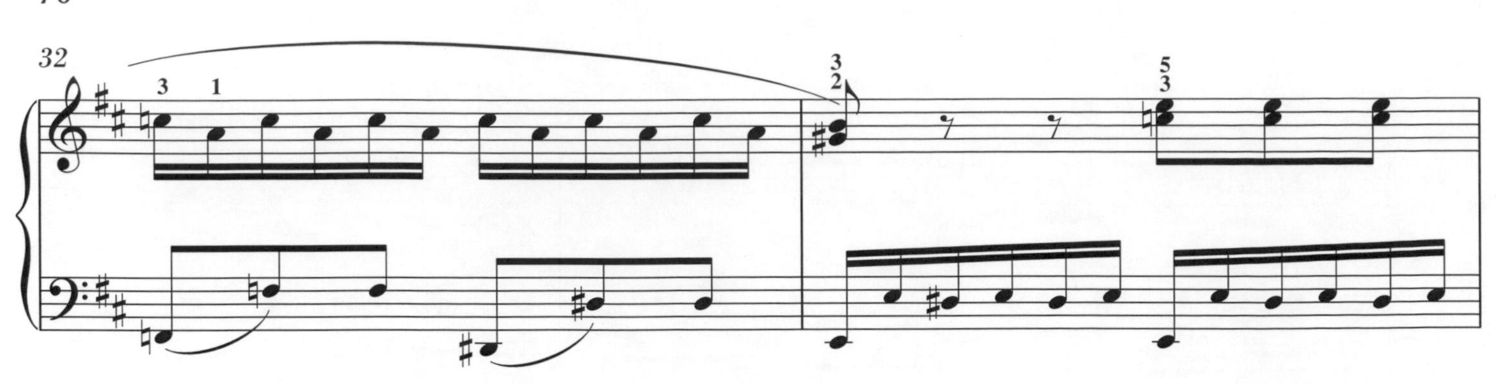

dim.
p

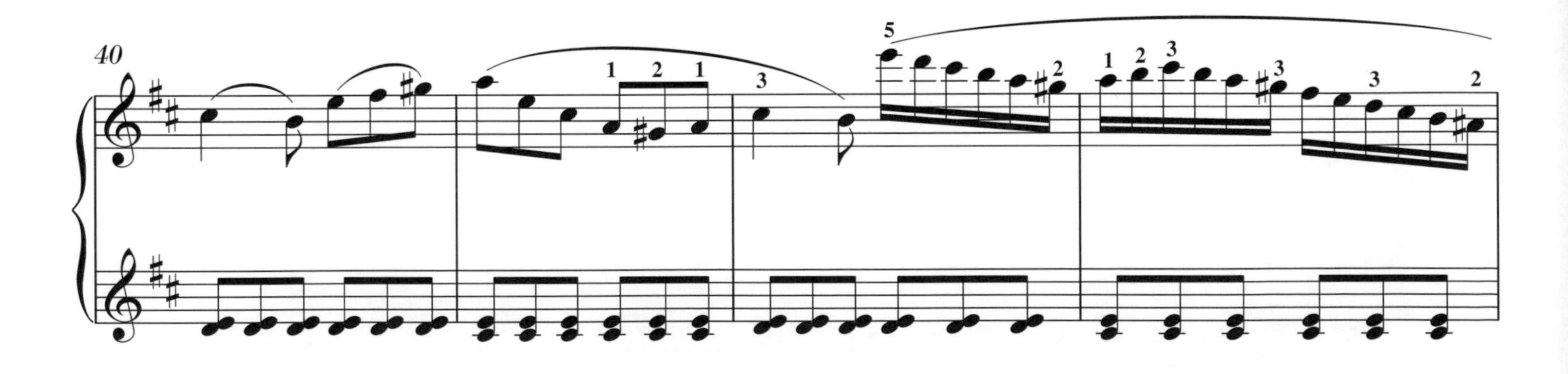

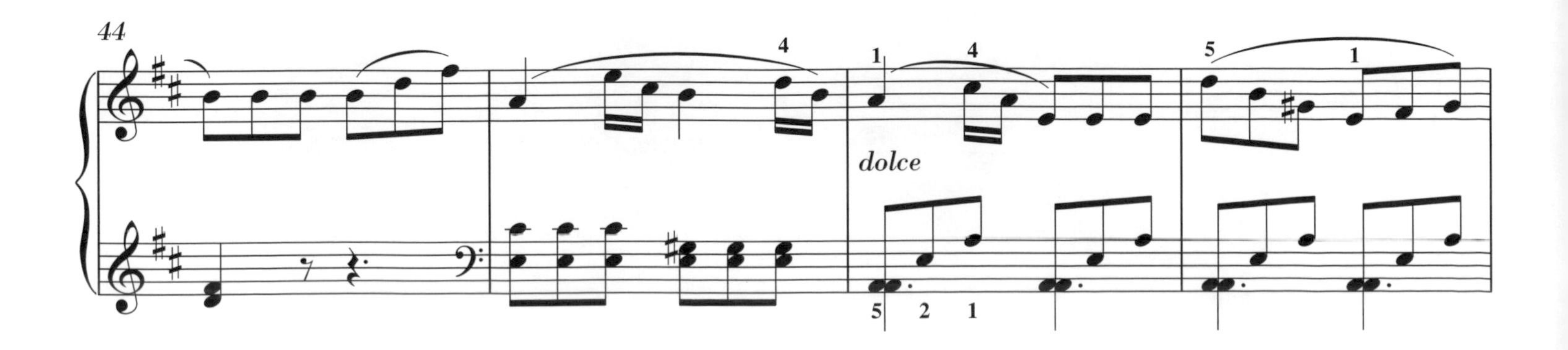
dolce

48

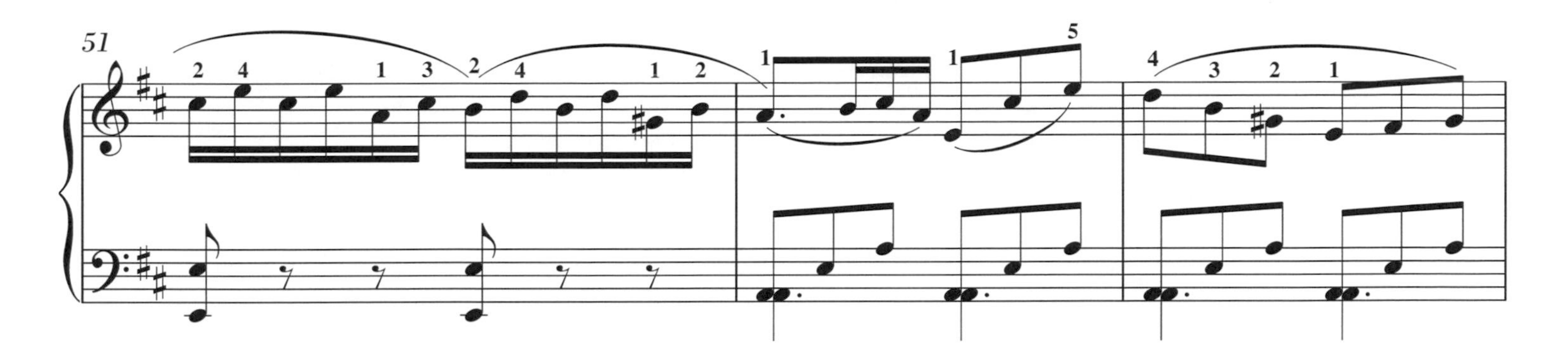
51

54
f

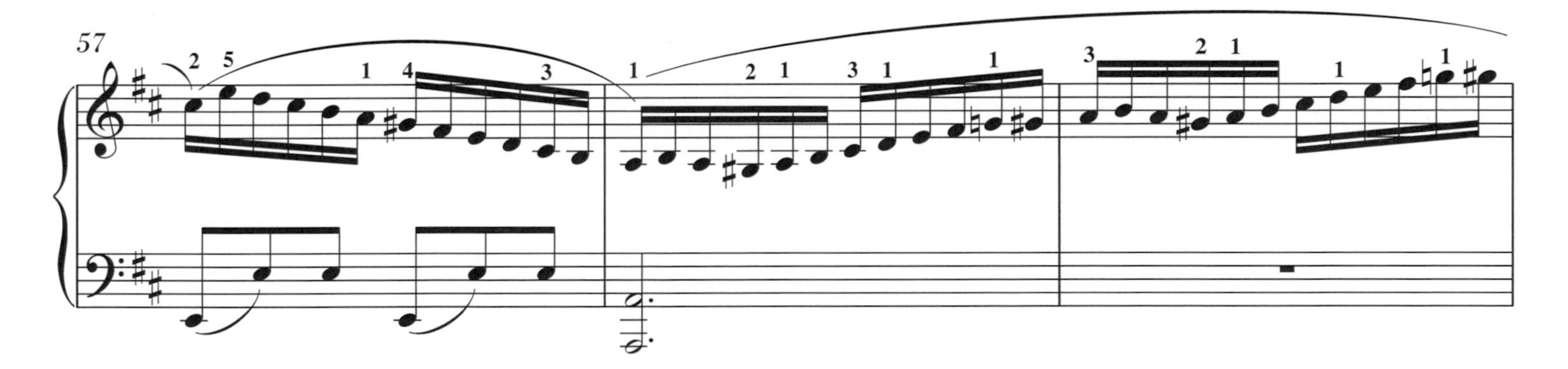
57

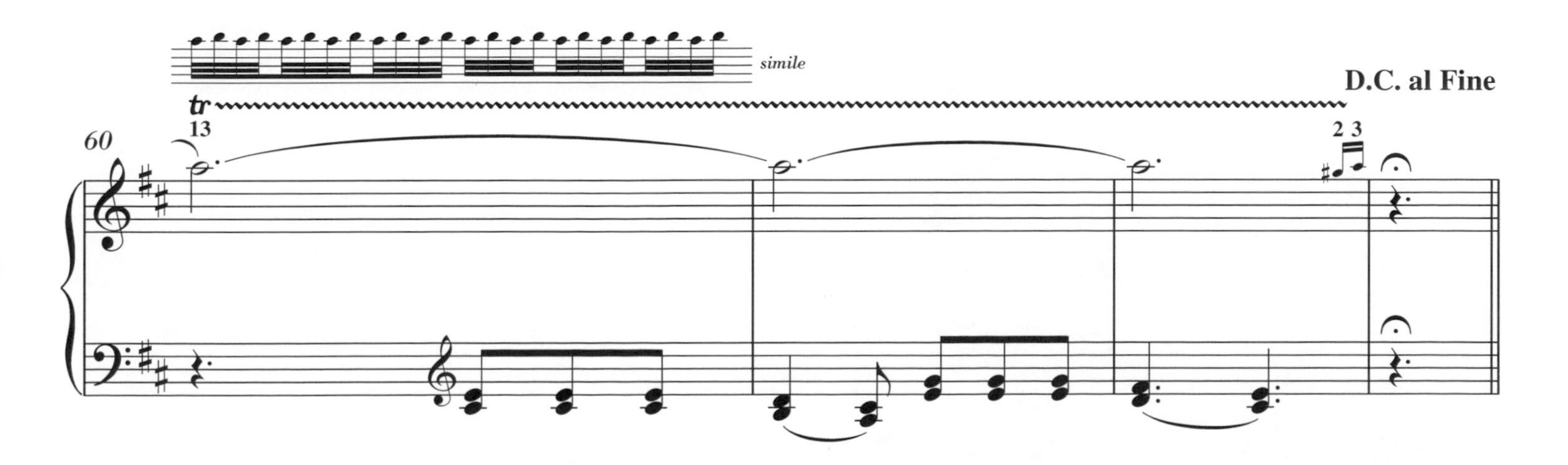
simile
D.C. al Fine
tr
60

ABOUT THE EDITOR

JENNIFER LINN

An accomplished pianist, teacher, and clinician in St. Louis, Missouri, Jennifer Linn is a contributing composer and arranger for the *Hal Leonard Student Piano Library*. Other work includes serving as Assistant Editor for the HLSPL Technique Classics *Hanon for the Developing Pianist* and *Czerny: Selections from the The Little Pianist, Opus 823*. Ms. Linn has taught piano privately for over twenty years, with students successfully competing in state and national level auditions.

She has presented recitals, workshops, master classes, and HLSPL showcases throughout the United States and Canada, including state and national Music Teachers National Association conventions, the National Federation of Music Clubs national convention, and the World Piano Pedagogy Conference. She frequently adjudicates both piano performance and composition events throughout the Midwest. Her compositions have been selected for the National Federation of Music Clubs' festival list and have been featured in *Keys* magazine. As an active member of the Missouri Music Teachers Association, she is the Composition Chairperson and previously served as Vice President of the St. Louis Area Music Teachers Association.

In 1999-2000, Ms. Linn served as Visiting Lecturer in Piano Pedagogy at the University of Illinois at Urbana-Champaign and has been on the faculty for the Illinois Summer Youth Music Piano Camp since 1998. Ms. Linn received her B.M. and M.M. in Piano Performance from the University of Missouri-Kansas City (UMKC) Conservatory of Music where she was the winner of the Concerto-Aria Competition. She was also awarded the prestigious Vice Chancellor's Award for Academic Excellence and Service.